The Three Realities

"He has no sense of reality."

"But which reality are you speaking of ?"

First reactions

"A manuscript bustling with ideas."
Jean-Pierre Cohen-Addad, University Professor Emeritus, Physics, Grenoble, author.

"This is a fascinating text."
Jean-Charles Stasi, journalist, author.

To my children Emeric and Laetitia

The Three Realities

physical, perceived, represented
here, now, evolutions

Xavier BOLOT

Translator Mandy Brice

Published by
Mandrake
PO Box 250
OXFORD
OX1 1AP (UK)

By the same author

Drawing in real perspective, a new approach to space, natural and immediate application, Mandrake, 2017.

Neutral Light, a new approach to drawing and painting brought by XXIth century science, L'Harmattan, 2009.

How to represent action, the pleasure of applying life sciences to live arts, L'Harmattan, 2012.

Contents

Realities and Truth

Powerful institutions want us to believe their truths, and in order to achieve this, they standardize language. Thus social conventions for representing the world only reflect one aspect of things. Moreover, as time goes by, people and their institutions, their customs, their beliefs and their truths, come and go. Therefore the irreplaceable truth of today and now is an illusion. We will leave these tricks to the illusionist politicians and those who are enthusiasts for the notion of the existence of the back-world of metaphysics.

Indeed, we live on Earth with three realities: physical, perceived and represented. We observe that our perceptions are illusions, that our representations are fantasies, and that we are ourselves the physical world. It is only natural, as we have a left brain and a right brain, it anticipates, it is geared towards action, and consequently we have survived.

Is this really that complicated? Perhaps, but we must take into consideration the fact that we function like that: our body acts and our brain fantasizes.

Perhaps some of our convictions will crumble, perhaps we will need courage to face this new universe, but we are going to gain a new research tool.

At the end of the day the three realities will seem like sources of balanced thought in a thorough and fresh approach which will afford us the richest and least incomplete view of things possible.

I have already approached this notion of three realities in my three previous publications. I have demonstrated the mechanism of perspective such as we perceive it; I have indicated the neutral character of light and I have put forward a process for the representation of action.

Yet, in the course of things I have been able to observe, by refocusing notions as fundamental as emotion or consciousness in the light of neuroscience, to what extent our beliefs in a truth remain entrenched. A belief that has the specific feature of being logically and totally unjustified, and therefore ineradicable by reason. Indeed, such belief is part of our identity.

Taking a belief away from someone amounts to the same thing as disorientating and destroying them psychologically. This explains many violent and incomprehensible clan and religious wars. Only in death can Romeo and Juliet be together again or war enable Palestinians and Jews to be honoured on the same land. Unless a political power decides otherwise, as when King Henry IV declared "Paris is well worth a mass."

Belief often makes it possible to organize our life without thinking too much. The religions of the Book emphasize the faithful. They cultivate the image of a father, saviour of the child, deprived of physical strength, of experience, of knowledge and of judgement. The believer is infantilized to the extent that he or she is unable to see what is right in front of their eyes.

Our western culture is still profoundly impregnated with traces of religions of the Book which makes little effort to represent the complexity of the world. Mao's *Little Red Book*, contained the "Truth", one and inescapable, that in the hands of those who possess the meaning, carefully maintain total power over minds and over bodies.

Yet it could be a different story if we think about it. Each of us knows that we have eyes to see, ears to hear, a nose to smell with, sensors to understand the surrounding nature in which our very substance is immersed and in constant exchange.

Our body is continually giving out and receiving energy. What can we perceive about the physical world surrounding us? By what means can I understand in other words, how can I represent - what I feel? How can I coherently communicate what I feel? Answering these questions is too complicated for the believer who doesn't want to be challenged. They prefer to remain blind, to let dogma replace their perception.

Perceived reality is what we have right in front of our eyes, whether we use a microscope, a telescope or a Geiger counter, or even have our eyes closed.

What then, is the physical object? The physical object whose very presence changes me chemically, like the blade of a knife, which, passing in front of my eyes, makes my heart beat faster?

Yet two people will not perceive the same blue, nor detect the same smell. I may never perceive exactly the same thing twice. I may find that water is hot after having my hands in cold water, and cold after having had my hands in tepid water.

There exists therefore a physical world that is different from our world of perception, and which, we know, is not always faithfully represented by our speech, drawings, or our gestures.

We live with three realities. We are not faced with one truth. In other words we face an inescapable conceptual relativism. These three realities are: physical reality, perceived reality and represented reality.

These remarks are deeply baffling for some people. I recall a journalist, looking worried, asking me questions such as "But where do you want this to lead us?". Or the first president of an appeals court to whom I demonstrated the curvilinear pillars of a cathedral, asked with a puzzled look: "Sir, tell me what I should be seeing."

I therefore thought it necessary to devote a publication to this issue of the three realities, so that it would be understood as a fundamental question, plain for all to see in their daily life. Optical illusions don't surprise psychologists or artists who are regularly confronted with these phenomena in their work. However, being aware of the reality to which I am referring allows me to avoid misunderstandings and fosters the expression and development of an idea.

Approach

I haven't tried to either cover or to deal with all the subjects in encyclopedic detail. I have rather tried to show, with simple language, a broad-based vision, enabling us to better situate ourselves and ask questions, ranging from the simple to the complex.

I haven't tried to *explain* everything, to remove the wrinkles and make everything smooth, a vain undertaking. I simply try to *involve* the reader, to set him or her in motion independently and to encourage an approach of perpetual discovery, and thereby to immerse them in life.

It is for this reason that the fourth part of this text is devoted to practical everyday or philosophic examples. I haven't written a novel that makes the hours pass sweetly. The present moment experienced with every fibre of our body is the most important and we can delight in our daily questioning of a life, which is constantly being renewed.

Upon reflection, the proposed paradoxes, the considerations alluded to, varying in origin but related, could be paradigms in the coming postmodern world. They will cause upheavals not unlike those that modernity provoked at the time of the Renaissance.

We are in effect witnessing the disappearance of a world of outdated institutions, of antiquated schools which continue to enact unsuitable laws for the city. These old, out of touch ideas, have a corrosive effect on our lives, leaving us in the grip of a strange nightmare.

That is why we must now embark on an exciting adventure, experiencing a new world with the energy of youth, which will take us towards new era of hope.

PART I
Our perceptions are illusions

"Vanity of vanities all is vanity"
Ecclesiastics, I.2.

Introduction
Our shifting reality

Some with mental illness, such as schizophrenics, are convinced that their visual or auditory hallucinations are real. They don't make the distinction between physical and perceived reality. They also seem unaware that their perceptions can be illusionary.

Similarly, in daily life the average person supposes that, in principle, what he sees, what he hears, what he feels, corresponds to a solid reality, an undeniable truth of things. Yet at the same time, he will be able to adapt to any changes in perception that challenge his representation of things, taking a new path and perceiving the new reality. His new reality will be a new interpretation of his perceptions, in other words a new representation of the world.

Perception takes place in the presence of an object. Representation is constructed in the absence of the object. Representation is built from perceptions, but also from other factors, like memory or purpose.

Illusions are inherent to our biological constitution and functioning. According to Spinoza, the purpose of our body is to persevere in its own being, in other words to survive in the best possible environment and conditions.

In this context, our visual system is not a photographic device. Our eye contains a lens, but our retina and visual system anticipate and transfigure the world, to bring about our life-saving actions.

Chapter 1
Natural causes of illusions

1.1   Man and his sensors

Protagoras (490-420 BCE) spent part of his life as Diogenes Laërtius's porter. He was a slave when Diogenes bought him after noticing his ability for tying and untying the loads he was carrying. Protagoras was a pupil of Diogenes and in his memoirs he left a few principles including "Man is the measure of all things" In saying that, Protagoras anticipated the reversal brought about by Kant which puts man in his finitude at the centre of the world, and in that sense, prepared the way for the phenomenologists.

Yet man is not standard, he is diverse. If I am the measure of all things, how can my measure, beginning from my perception of things, be like my neighbour's, who I know is so different from me?

I may well go into a cathedral or a museum and yet not understand anything, not see anything, because of my particular culture. It is indeed to this effect that groups of expert, multilingual guides are established, instructed on the history of art, to do tours of European sites for tourists, who come to learn how to see what they can't see, what they see in front of them and what they are trying to see.

The cathedral of Bourges is the young sister of the cathedral of Paris. Both cathedrals were built from very similar plans, the two Archbishops of Sully were brothers. As a result of the Paris construction, and in a new attempt at innovation, Bourges has the advantage of having neither transept nor piers, but a double set of flying buttresses to maintain the edifice. As a consequence, this architecture offers 21 metre high lateral naves with a striking optical effect. In fact the visitor does not see straight vertical pillars but curved pillars, converging and diverging towards the top. Consequently it must be noted that several realities exist, beginning with a physical reality of pillars built vertically and straight, and a perceived reality of pillars which we see curved.

This phenomenon can be commonly observed everywhere, more or less clearly depending on volume proportions, and particularly in streets in the centre of San Francisco or New York.

This perceptive phenomenon is due to our ocular system made up of two spherical eyes sufficiently close together for our visual world to be akin to a cylindrical surface.

We will come back to this shattering of reality, while bearing in mind that a book *"Drawing in real perspective"* has been devoted to this practical theme.

Hence there is a first practical cause for our perceptual illusions, those produced by our sensory sensors, whether they be sight, touch, sense of smell: the fact that we are human beings attempting to comprehend the world through the prism of our sensors.

Yet a number of other factors intervene which bring us specific, variable and changing information about the outside world.

1.2   The measures I take depend on algorithms

First of all, some measures are differential, that is to say they can only be comparative. I am blinded by daylight when I come back up from a dark cellar in which I could nevertheless discern objects perfectly.

When I am in a train at the station, I imagine that it is moving again whereas it is a nearby train which moves in the opposite direction, on the other side of the platform.

When a purple mark is next to an orange mark, the purple seems more blue and the orange seems more yellow.

Moreover we are very skillful at discerning an angle but not a distance. We can see immediately, to a quarter of a degree, if a frame on a wall is not horizontal, yet we make an error of almost twenty percent when we compare a vertical segment to a horizontal segment of the same physical length. The latter appears shorter to us.

At any rate, we imagine situations which don't reflect our sensations. I feel as if my hands are wet doing the washing up, whereas I am wearing gloves. In the fog, cars seem far from each other, whereas they are near, which is very dangerous. We have here an example of the system of perception that has evolved in conflict with good sense, with all due respect to finalistic and deterministic philosophers. As Pangloss already pointed out, the nose didn't grow on a face in order to put glasses on it, because glasses didn't exist.

1.3 The interaction of my body with the environment

1.3.1 I change chemically in the presence of the object

The living being, whether it be a simple cell or a complex body, is made up of an envelope and an internal medium. Its envelope is porous and a constant exchange of energy and chemical compounds takes place with its environment. Doors open and close depending on the needs of the living cell.

The effect of these exchanges is the constant maintenance of the internal medium's chemical parameters within a balanced range and in constant exchange with the outside. We all know that if our blood doesn't contain the right proportions of oxygen, potassium, sugar, fat etc., we risk death.

Thus any brutal modification in the environment can change my internal balance, such as a lack of oxygen, or poisonous gases, or when the outside temperature is such that I can get dehydrated, or on the contrary frozen etc., the same applies when an object suddenly appears in my environment.

Faced with the intrusion of any object, my brain gives an alarm, my adrenal glands release adrenalin, my heart starts beating wildly, my hands become clammy and a series of internal measures are implemented.

1.3.2 The perceived object is therefore no longer the same

Having been chemically changed under the effect of the adrenalin, my organism will no longer perceive the same things in the same way. I will no longer be interested in the same details of the object. I want to know if the thing is a slow-worm at a standstill or a sleeping adder. I will search my memory for the colours of both animals, their size, the shape of their heads.

Depending on these results I will adopt a strategy of escape, attack, or waiting. Depending on my character and my experience, responses of fear may or may not arise. If I had been less emotional, I would have realised at once that it was a twisted piece of wood. The object is no longer the same and I recover my inner equilibrium, my breathing goes back to normal, my heart calms down.

The state of my body influences my perception. A headache prevents me from tolerating too bright a light, growing old makes objects seem blurry, the colours change, and to be convinced of this one merely has to look at Cézanne or Picasso's later canvases to realise that their painter's palette had changed.

1.3.3 This causes a group effervescence phenomenon

The object which has intruded on my field of perception is not merely inert: I can in fact receive mineral compounds such as naphthalene or organic compounds such as human odours or female or male pheromones. This phenomenon is accelerated by the presence of mirror neurons around Broca's area and in the lower parietal cortex. These neurons also exhibit activity when an animal or human individual carries out an action only when he observes another individual carry out the same action, or even when he imagines such an action, hence the term *mirror*.

My body changes chemically. This means that, in meeting the Other, their body will also change chemically. And my perception will in turn change and I will perceive a new Other. And the phenomenon will be recurring and cumulative.

This can be commonly observed between two people when tension or anger mounts, or in a football stadium during a match when the crowd can be seen getting up and cheering as one single voice in a collective effervescence phenomenon.

1.4 Focusing attention

We can only see part of the scenery surrounding us. An object that you are fascinated with can seem oversized or of an extraordinary colour.

Inversely. we can experience mental blindness. Pilots in a training room are not able to see a camel crossing the runway where they are landing, given that the presence of this animal is incongruous and unlikely in a northern country.

You are looking for a friend's lighter who tells you on the telephone that she had left it at your place on the occasion of dinner the previous day. The lighter is on the table in front of you, yet you can't see it because it is blue whereas you thought it was red.

A number of mental blindness experiments have shown that the fact of having a shattered windscreen makes you lose sight of the white line in the middle of the road or important elements of the road landscape.

Similarly, we can shut out surrounding background noise when we are following a conversation. In fact, our body produces these phenomena naturally, which are illusions to our perception, but which are not illusions to our body which only takes useful elements into consideration for the purpose of survival.

Chapter 2
Constructed illusions

A number of artists and psychologists have been experimentally interested in the construction of optical effects that result in different kinds of illusions or questions from the reader.

2.1 Indecision

Thus the illusion of Isia Leviant (1914-2006) gives the impression of a vibrant, revolving circle. The perception phenomenon would come from the intense random activity in the occipital V2 area.

The illusion of the cube of crystallographer L.A. Necker (1786-1861) is interesting as it highlights a phenomenon which we experience frequently: hesitation in deciding what object is there in front of us. When we don't have all the elements to make a decision, we can see alternatively one image and then another, faced with an object, our brain hesitates between two possible solutions.

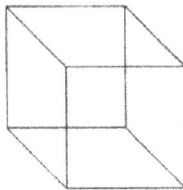

In this regard with Salvador Dali's (1904-1989) "*Slave market with the disappearing bust of Voltaire*" we are able to see alternatively, either the bust of Voltaire, or two peasant women.

2.2 Anticipation

At any rate, optical illusions relating to our constant extrapolation activity are amazing. They are the most interesting of visual illusions because they highlight our constant extrapolation activity, which has enabled us to survive the course of the development of animal species. When we are faced with danger or an anomaly, we immediately imagine scenarios in which we make the right decision to survive, even before having all the information to hand. Time is of the essence.

The most spectacular visual expression of our aptitude to anticipate is our ability to manufacture virtual characteristics. These virtual characteristics are produced by neurons from neuronal columns in the occipital VI area of vision.

That is why Kanisza's triangle and its variants are completed by our imagination from a simple clue placed at the top of each.

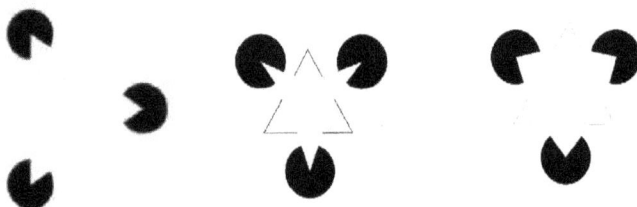

The white triangles, virtual yet perceived, are whiter than the sheet of paper, and the more we look at them, the whiter they become. This means that the anticipation phenomenon intensifies.

This anticipatory activity is fundamental in documenting decision-making. The angle drawn at the ends being 60°, we can see a triangle with rectilinear sides. If the angle is larger we can see a concave curvilinear triangle, and if the triangle is smaller, a convex curvilinear triangle.

2.3 Memory

Memory plays a large role in perception. For example, when I look at the clouds and in them see shapes of fantastic animals, when I meet a friend, when I watch puppets at a Punch and Judy show, when I hear footsteps which remind me of my father's, or when the sight of an object suddenly evokes before me part of my past.

Perception and memory are attributed to the brain's emotional limbic area. The perception of an object disturbs my inner chemical balance, that is to say it provokes an emotion, which is itself recorded in my brain at the time of so-called episodic memorization.

According to Serge Laroche, the recording process uses certain genes, in particular the *Zif268* gene, whose task is to sustainably develop neuronal synaptic terminations of the image to be recorded.

2.4 Loss of reference points

Perception can lose its reference points in some cases of a change in familiar environmental conditions. Thus the observation of a Walt Disney drawing with coloured lighting completely transforms the colours of the poster, causing the fox to lose its characteristic red coat.

A drawing can correspond to an impossible object when certain indications are not coherent with the knowledge of the brain that is observing it.

The colours of a painting can irradiate the whole in parts where the painter has put no colour. In 1971, Dario Varin brought to light this illusion which he called "the neon effect" .

The Weiskrantz refinery. It is the nickname given by Weiskrantz to a work of the graphic representation of perception feedback loops in cynomolgus monkeys.

A grey netting in the middle of a black netting gives the impression of a large grey area, as Jacques Ninio from the Physical Statistic Laboratory of the Paris Ecole Normale Supérieure illustrated.

A dismantled chair, seen from a certain angle, can give the impression of being a normal chair, making it possible to pass someone through the chair.

2.5 The complexity of perception

A map of different fields of vision was drawn in the 1990s thanks to the works of Ungerleider and Mishkin, then Van Essen and Felleman. These multiple connections between 32 areas allow us to understand how, according to Felleman, 80% of the fibres which arrive in the occipital areas of vision, V1 to V4, don't come from the eye. In fact, we know that our visual perception depends on a great number of factors such as our culture, our intentions of action, our preconceived idea of an aim to be reached and, in general, our activity of constant mental anticipation and reconstruction of the world.

Remarks on the Part I
A strange perception of the world

We notice first of all that our perception of the physical world doesn't correspond either automatically or compulsorily to the physical reality that surrounds us and which forms us, in as much as we know anything about the physical reality of things.

We are dependent on the nature of our sensors as well as on the way our internal calculators work and the reliability of our memories. Our measurements are not always trustworthy and the interpretation of these measurements is tainted by emotion, in other words the degree of intensity of disturbances brought to our inner balance which we call homeostasis.

What matters is that this system enables us to survive in an environment subject to the constant chance of nature. *This perceived reality is mine*, it allows me to survive, for what more can I ask, ponders the artist ?

Physical reality is, however, the aim of a physician's research, who, through his corporal sensors and tools has been able to make, will and endeavour to collect still more information about the strange physical world, and in this way it will always hold new surprises for us.

Curiously the physicist describes this world with the help of the ritual formula "*Everything happens as if*", which belongs to the imaginary world, to the world of fairytales, to the world of poets.

Admittedly the scientist will be careful to check that the measurements he takes are coherent with his last fairytale, but the abstractions evoked, presuppositions, simple childish mechanical images proposed, are summoned to reinforce the very serious narration of the scholar.

Hard physics navigates in a magical world, in pursuit of a living reality, evolutionary and multiple. Inversely, man who has attempted to explain his presence on earth, started by inventing sacred mythologies and fantastic representations, but without the worry of confronting them experimentally and systematically in the physical world.

The schizophrenic believer is thus disconnected from the perceived environment and from his brothers. He sees a world built from a back-world. He has provoked the biggest massacres in the name of abstract ideas: power, money, class superiority, or other terms expressing his existential anxiety. Whatever his shifting reality, it is for him a source of worry more comfortably replaced by a single, intangible, unchanging and eternal truth.

The believer goes on a crusade to shape the world to his advantage. He exhibits the behaviour of a looter. He is antisocial. At the tribal level, the behaviour is of the same nature as when we see people cutting each other's throats on a world stage. The living being, right from the time of the living cell, is a predator by design.

Part II:
Our representations are fantasies

Introduction
Our inevitable fantasies

We very often ignore the origins of our fantasies. They may have been conceived unconsciously but also consciously. Self-reflection is necessary to rediscover elements stored in our bodies which were used in the construction of fantasy. It is not an easy thing, as our neuronal activity is constant and random.

Moreover, our representations can only be transmitted to the Other by our means of communication, in other words gesture, demeanour, facial expressions, dilation of our pupils, the opening of our eyelids, colour changes in our skin, the bristling of our hairs, our trembling, the hormones we secrete, the tone of our voice, and finally speech.

Our gesture may be in total contradiction to our speech. A clan chief approaches a sworn enemy with clenched fists, although the intention is to congratulate. A shopkeeper states to a customer that his order will be fulfilled, all the while scratching his head.

We are going to see, therefore, with a few examples, that our communication is physical and that it is established by our gestures, our lips, our eyes. The language of deaf-mutes is eloquent: it is composed of hand and arm gestures and all sorts of mimicking.

The brain only intervenes with speech after the battle with a prefabricated, cumbersome arsenal. Speech is slow and poorer, which doesn't help us to clarify the content of our fantasies. The reception and transmission of sounds are made to the rhythm of several dozens of bits per second, whereas images offers millions of pixels per second, in the knowledge that our visual system only receives a part.

Eventually we notice that in every case our fantasies have been generated by random neuronal activity, with a left brain for speech, which functions to express our representations or our messages, without taking into consideration the sensitive right brain, in contact with physical reality.

We will examine the substrates of consciousness and sub-consciousness, in this random universe

Chapter 1
The concrete and the imaginary
– what Kant didn't know

The construction of our body submits to the laws of chance, from gene chains, to the behaviour of the environment. This results in a biological cobbling-together which means that our brain in particular was developed in successive layers, each at a different speed. Our reflection is not synchronous with our action. Our awareness of a phenomenon, and our physical action faced with this phenomenon, is not synchronous. The body, as far as our nervous system and our brain are concerned, contribute to the establishment of actions, adapted to circumstances, which may be complex.

1.1   Our gesture is true,
our perception is false

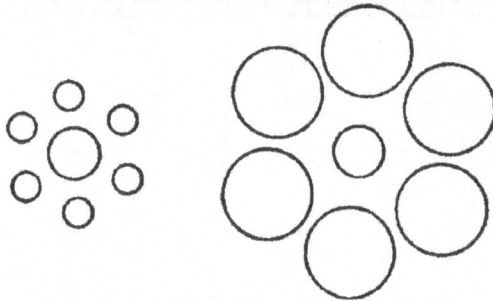

Titchener's (1867-1927) illusion consists of presenting a circle surrounded by small circles and, in another image, the same circle surrounded by large circles. We know that our visual system gives us differential information, namely comparatives. We are therefore not surprised to perceive the central circle smaller when it is surrounded by large circles and larger when it is surrounded by small circles.

Only here is something to be surprised about: In 1995, Aglioti had the idea, to ask an observer to grasp the central circle with his fingers. He was able to observe that the opening between the thumb and the index finger, from the start of the arm movement, in trying to pinch the object, was correctly adjusted to the physical dimension of the central disc, whether it be for the image on the left or the right.

Thus the visual-motor order was correct, as soon as the order was registered, as soon as the beginning of the arm movement, whereas we are convinced that we are dealing with two central circles of different sizes. We are fooled by our perceptions, whereas our body's motor system doesn't make mistakes.

Our corporal actions are reliable, our perception of things are not. A physico-chemical exchange took place with our outside environment, whatever the failings of our perceptive imagination, otherwise our body wouldn't survive, if it fed itself with illusions.

Contrary to what Kant (1724-1804) says, the physical world is not out of reach. Neuroscience shows us, on the contrary, in this simple example, direct physical exchange can exist between my body and the physical world.

To reconcile the two statements, on one hand Kantian and on the other hand neuro-scientific, we must be able to distinguish between the perceived world and the physical world, and to consider them as complimentary.

We can understand that Kant says the physical object is inaccessible to his understanding and to his senses. But we know that a physicist, in taking measurements, presupposes that physical reality is accessible, and by constant physical symbiotic exchange of the living being with its environment.

What is happening? We have just seen, above, the multiple loops of Weiskrantz's *refinery*. The neurologists Ungerleider and Mishkin have shown that all those connections between the eye and the occipital area are organized into two main pathways: ventral and dorsal. The ventral pathway is for the description of shapes and colours, whereas the dorsal is the pathway of movement and action.

These two pathways, as we have just seen, don't provide the same results. We have here the example of our bodies, not very coherent construction.

The two needs of vision and action existed, but also evolved through a random biological cobbling-together over millions of years. We live symbiotically with the physical world, like bacteria, which don't have neurons, a nervous system, or, a brain. In addition, we have a brain, which has developed at its own pace, and at different paces for different parts, which are not always consistent between each other or with the rest of the body.

This autonomous development of the brain has been very well illustrated by the works of Didier Marchand on the evolution of the brain in cetaceans derived from an otter returned to the ocean, and on its consequences on the shape and position of the skull in relation to the spinal column.

1.2 Gesture intervenes 55 milliseconds before awareness of gesture

Suddenly I take my hand away from a hot plate which had been on a fire. I wanted to pick the plate up. I don't notice its colour, or the vibrations in the air around it. Too late! I burnt myself. Fortunately, I withdrew my hand immediately. My fingers are sore now. I hastily put my hand under a tap of cold water to relieve the pain.

55 milliseconds- or half a tenth of a second elapsed, (which is enormous under such circumstances) before I understood what had taken place, when I became aware of the situation. Everything is over. My hand is burnt. Yet the immediate and unconscious body reflex reaction enabled me to act urgently and limit the damage.

It should be noted that a considerable number of snakes detect infrared radiation in their prey through detector cells situated under their noses. We are not equipped with such a device. The cobbling-together of evolution decided it thus.

1.3 We are betrayed by our smile

Our inner balance is indispensable to our survival. During a disturbance in our environment, emotion becomes a combination of unconscious reactions & physico-chemical adjustments in our body.

Emotion is useful because it manages the first instants of an alert, it allows an easier and more sustainable storage of information in long-term memory, and allows us to recall new facts more easily. Visceral information plays a large part in emotion.

The subconscious triggering of emotions explains why it is difficult to simulate them voluntarily, and easy to identify when they are fake. This is the difference between a spontaneous smile, triggered by the limbic system, which is always dissymmetric, and a conscious, symmetric, business-like smile, triggered by the motor cortex activating the zygomatic muscles.

The large zygomatic is a cheek muscle which goes down from the malar bone towards and into the corner of the mouth. This is why the tilt of the mouth and the direction of the corner of the mouth, send us such a clear signal.

From our early childhood, we have learned to read our mother's lips. When we listen to someone against intrusive background music, we need to follow the movement of the lips. We do the same when we listen to an English teacher. It is easier for us to follow a filmed rather than an audio-recorded conversation.

All in all, by a deliberate smile, I project an image which is not the one I would like to give.

1.4 My eye "speaks" first

We have seen that we have two visual pathways a ventral one: processing shapes and colours, the other dorsal, processing movement; for example, the position of a tennis ball in relation to its surroundings. The dorsal pathway is concerned with the object's field of action and not the shape of the object. It informs my motor system, which reacts subconsciously. It is essential in combat.

This dorsal pathway uses the superior colliculus, the pulvinar, ending in the posterior parietal cortex, which participates in sending motor information. However, this pathway uses low frequencies transmitted to the amygdala, which reacts to frightened faces.

Paul Whalen noticed that the amygdala's signal for fright is simply the whites of the eyes. This process is totally subconscious. When afraid I easily betray myself, information which is highly interesting to my opponent, who takes advantage because he knows that I am not in full command of my faculties. We find once more the cobbling-together, the random construction of evolution, bearer of advantages and disadvantages.

Eckhard H. Hess has shown that pupil dilation increases in front of something stimulating, when asked to observe food, politicians, or music. We can also observe an increase in the size of the pupil in the solving of a problem and, in particular, at the point of finding the solution.

Someone who is lying and doesn't want to betray himself looks away. "Look at me" means "Listen to me and I'll be able to see what you are thinking."

Looking out of the corner of the eye can mean several different things depending on the context: defiance, seduction. The expression is composed of the eye and its facial or gestural context, or odours or sounds produced.

A look up to the right indicates thought. A look down, submission. Sustaining a look is insolence. Rolling the eyes means "I don't understand anymore, I no longer know where to look." A look can be a weapon. The politician Georges Marchais baffled journalists seated in front of him by his constant revolving and haunting look that showed a cornea instead of an iris. That is why the television screen only shows this politician face exceptionally and in pre-recorded declarations. Our facial expression can be unwittingly thoughtful, lost or in attendance.

Chapter 2
The indigence of language

In comparison to the rapidity and reliability of our body's reactions, today's speech tool is really onerous. Codification brought by the written word has introduced a considerable number of constraints without reducing conversational shortcomings.

On the receptive side, the eye rapidly scans a very large amount of information, the ear has much more inertia and only receives low speed input, and speech utilizes a cumbersome mechanism, which can only be produced slowly.

This is why, during a conversation, the orator's words may frequently be cut by the interlocutor's brain, which has had time to deal with the situation thanks to body language, information previously stored in memory, and the first remarks registered and dealt with.

2.1 Living Tribal Semantics

Tribal language was simple in its emergence, "rhythmic, bilateral and three-phrased" according to the anthropologist Marcel Jousse. Animal language has always been at a distance, an out of sight call or alert means of communication.

Each cry means something precise and is considered as a learning process by the Canadian wolf or the verve monkey from Kenya. These animals have a conscience. In other words, they establish a relationship between their body and the environment, where the latter manifests itself in variations, for example by the apparition of an object or the presence of the Other.

Each tribe has its language, and this language evolves continuously according to the needs of the tribe. The Academy, in keeping with central authority built upon scattered tribes, has continued to enact rules, but it sees itself in turn restricted to constantly updating its vocabulary under pressure from mutations in language. Standardization always lags behind life.

Large sections of society express themselves without any approved speaking standards. New dialects are born and spread through multiple communities that want to experience their identity as expressed by their customs.

2.2 Word polysemy

The significance of language to my *tribe* is here and now. It will not have the same meaning tomorrow, or elsewhere. It will adapt to constant exchanges of my body with its new environment. Yet I will always have past emotions in my memory. One word may evoke several memories.

This word, *today*, carries meaning for me, which may not be shared by my friends. We are in a constant learning mode, like a child who discovers the meaning of words from the context in which he finds himself. One word may have a very precise meaning when it is put in its place in a traditional phrase, in an expression known to my tribe.

Learning a language via columns of vocabulary learnt by heart has been shown to be ineffective. Language learning takes place in simple scenarios, learning phrases in which there is a subject, an action, and an object. The language then finds its usefulness in solving a communication problem; vocabulary and syntax acting together.

Word polysemy becomes more disturbing when I describe a scenario that I have imagined to represent a perception. Each representation is indeed my representation, my invention that hasn't yet been standardized in society's little roleplays.

How is it possible to access a new mental construction with poor material, uncertain measurements, composed of matter, which still holds on to its secrets? That certainly doesn't simplify things, because the new representation that I have just discovered results from a piece of random neuronal work.

2.3 Ambiguities in syntax

When the animal, in a broader sense, including man, is not in the present of the action, but in the memory of the action, he must, according to Marcel Jousse (1886-1961) relate the "three-phasism" of the agent, the action and the object. In other words he must construct the first articulation of subject-verb-direct object.

Syntax was complicated, and leisurely, in libraries, which are closed places, where writing requires standards, bearers of hope for communication, spreading over time and space.

Yet all over the world, writing was the privilege of a dominant class. Over time, several generations having past, writing rapidly became illegible, for most readers who abandoned this skill to archivists of a bygone area.

It should be noted that to understand writings which have become enigmas, researchers must not only know the signals used, but the history and geography surrounding them. Nevertheless, primitive

THE THREE REALITIES   C3 43

three-phasism actor-action-effect will always have existed and subsisted in nature. But the declensions and conjugations from bygone eras have disappeared along with the customs and people who used them.

2.4 Incompleteness of evolutive logic

We must not forget that language presupposes logic. But must the logic of this language always correspond to mine? Logic evolves with language. Different logics come into being every day in mathematical theories and we have already seen several logics clashing in modern physics. Logic is built on a number of assumptions, on identities and relationships between these identities.

Bachelard underlined that the notion of logic is a perpetual construction. On the knowledge front, scientists sense the limits of their logics.

Euclide, father of plane geometry, Pythagorus of trigonometry, Bayes of probability, Boole of information technology logic, Gödel the limits and contradictions of arithmetic, Riemann complex cosmic spaces, Connes, operator algebra to explore quantum physics, have all been confronted with new phenomena leading them to research new logic. Logic is only a means of scientific or philosophical thinking. Other means of thinking exist, other means of decision-making than that of the logical domain. We are entering into the world of intuition and bright ideas in artistic and scientific fields arising from chance.

Our language is an unsophisticated communication device, and slow, leading us to respect the most elementary basic logic, common to the largest number, in an attempt to communicate. Hence the interminable contradictions of speech when attempting to express with words what is indescribable.

Speech enables, as much as a go-between's work, the composition of impenetrable screens in our own minds. According to Bergson, language is incapable of describing complexity, mobility, humanity's reality. Language is polysemic and takes us where we don't want to go.

We think we have analyzed our sentiment by translating it into words, except we substituted a juxtaposition of inert states. Thus the notion of duration, lived experience, non-measurable, can only be replaced by the notion of linear and mathematical time, transmitted by language.

Lived experience is indescribable. Through Damasio's work, neuroscientists now know that we can't continue reasoning without the action of our emotional limbic brain.

Chapter 3
Unrestrained neuronal combinatorics

3.1 Thought, decision, consciousness

Thought is a group of cerebral activities, which are expressed in decision, planning, perception, and representation. These activities can take place consciously or unconsciously. The substrates of these activities are distributed throughout the body and brain. Different parts of the brain can be activated by constant random activity in the grey matter or, on the contrary, contain so-called encapsulated units which carry out irrepressible and subconscious tasks. These can be very elaborate tasks, such as recognizing a letter of the alphabet, irrespective of the calligraphy used.

How is this complex group organized? Many works allow us to describe thought organization schematically in simple and concrete terms, without being excessive.

So then how do we function physically in our uncertain universe? Society has always tended to represent a random phenomenon, wind for example, with a deterministic image, for example the god Eole of the ancient Greeks. In fact, without determinism, imagined and accepted by our species, anticipation of actions would not be possible, nor would the species survive.

To this purpose of anticipation, our imaginative subconscious constantly extrapolates new representations, new neuronal combinations, the most unlikely new scenarios of the unexpected, generated by our body's exchanges with its natural and social environment. Chance is physically present everywhere, it is our richness, and it engenders our specificity in the absence of any causality. Neither the construction of living organisms, as Jacques Monod showed, nor their everyday biological functioning, as Jean-Jacques Kupiec showed, escape chance.

So how does the living being develop? According to de Duve, the living being, in order to develop, has to attribute its complexity by exporting its entropy, that is to say its quantity of disorder, into its environment. The living being is always off balance. In developing in this way, in detriment to its immediate circle, the living being appears essentially as a predator, of which nature is the source of its social and environmental behaviour.

So how does the living being function? The living being is composed of a porous frontier and an internal medium in constant dynamic balance with the outside. This internal balance is called our homeostatic balance, from the Greek *homoios*, " similar" and hístemi " static".

When you receive the results of your blood test you see a list of glucose so much, red globules so many, etc., and in the right-hand margin, a range of values within which each of the analyzed parameters should be found.

This set of ranges describes the homeostatic range within which your parameters should be found. We are now ready to propose a definition of emotion; we are going to do this by asking the question:

How do we perceive things? Emotion is simply the expression of a disturbance in the homeostatic balance. This disturbance may be provoked by a modification in the environment and in particular by the sudden entrance of an object in the environment.

In fact, the presence of the Object changes me chemically. Therefore, a sudden threat triggers the production of hormones and neurotransmitters in my body. These accelerate my heartbeat, distribute my blood in favour of my skeleton muscles, release glucose, accelerate my reflexes, concentrate my attention, stop my digestion, inhibit pain, make blood-clotting easier and increase the number of my lymphocytes, these last two factors allow me to repair possible injuries. It is marvelous.

In this example, chemical changes make me fit for combat. The sole presence of the Object has changed me chemically and engendered an energetic alteration.

So my modified self sees the Object differently, it sees a modified Object and this modified Object, in turn, modifies me. And so we can witness a recurring and cumulative phenomenon.

By this emotional approach, at first sight reductionist, we are, in fact, in a position to situate certain concepts that we nevertheless use regularly, yet not always well, when discerning outlines.

Let us therefore look at notions of attention and awareness, which are at the heart of perception.

Following an alert triggered by the amygdale, attention consists *of a state of brain activation* by molecules produced by the brain stem. These molecules known as transmitters will inundate most of the brain and in particular the control panels known as registers of Self, of the Object, and of Consciousness, which has been activated.

The registers of Self are in the deep layers, they follow the parameters of different parts of the body.

The registers of the Object correspond to information passing through the sensori-motor areas. These registers constantly supervise my body's physical interaction with the environment.

What are registers of consciousness? Consciousness is a relationship between Me and the Object. The registers of consciousness are registers in the deep, primitive layers, which link the registers of Self and the registers of the Object. Animals are therefore conscious.

In this linking, I am aware of something, at the same time as I know that it is me who perceives this thing.

This then is a new, considerable split in our dualistic beliefs, namely the idea that the functioning of our substrates do indeed correspond to our subjective observations.

3.2 States of consciousness

It is important to note four interesting points which will allow us to understand what happens in the performing arts, which consist, for example, of drawing dancers in the act of dancing.

The trance first appears as a simple focusing of attention on a real or virtual object. The trance then becomes a common phenomenon that is not out of the ordinary.

Subsequently, consciousness having been activated by neurotransmitters, explains why the same areas of the brain can function either in conscious mode or unconscious mode, or with

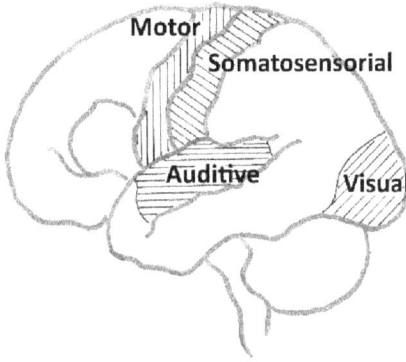

Registers of the Object (According to Damasio)

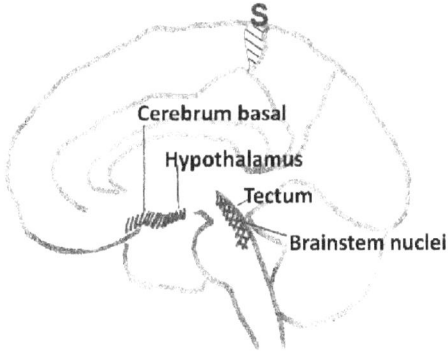

Registers of Self

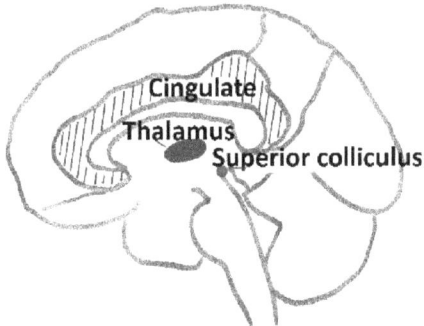

Registers of Consciousness

different states of consciousness of varying intensity, which can work at the same time.

These different states of consciousness are of varying intensity, but also of varying complexity, ranging from the core awareness of primitive animals, to the extended comprehensive awareness of evolved animals, which take into consideration the past history of the subject.

At any rate, the reality of random physical chemistry enables us to understand why our attention and our awareness appear or disappear in a whimsical fashion. Whereas our unconscious imagination, does not cease to function, because an unrestrained neuronal activity is releasing constant information, preparing the intention of an action in the same way as our poetic inspiration.

And now that we are equipped with enhanced concepts allowing us to better understand by which physical states and by which states of perception a designer or group of artists pass through, we can understand how to represent dancers in the act of dancing.

How can a relationship between the world perceived by my Self interacting with its environment, and the world represented by my past history be created? Knowing that the perceived world expresses itself in perceived time, whereas the represented world expresses itself in mathematical time, does not make things easy. Especially since live arts are performed precisely in this relationship between the perceived world and the represented world.

Well then, in our random physical and perceived worlds, to represent dancers in the act of dancing, the artist will have no other choice than to unwind, in successive instants on paper, the time elapsing here and now, time experienced in its constant unconscious activity, at random, with its subjective perceptions

Drawing is therefore neither the photograph of an attitude seized in passing, nor, as Duchamp had thought. the reproduction of a series of stills.

Hip Hop Street Dancer 1 24.04.2013. Live sketch. Felt tip pen on ordinary white A4 80g paper. Xavier Bolot.
This drawing is neither a photo nor a series of stills.

Live drawing is something else, an arm at a given time, a leg at another point in time, a head at yet another point in time, etc. expressing the living being off balance, such as we perceive it. It then becomes possible, by unfolding time, to draw a thumbnail sketch of dancers in the act of dancing or acrobats in action, to leave their traces on a piece of paper for the reader's appreciation. Indeed, right from the start of the creation of the drawing, the brain, anticipator of the Other of my tribe, is capable of reconstructing the scenario experienced, and recorded by the illustrator.

Communication has been initiated. The Other interprets my traces in an active reading. The porous characteristic of my drawing enables him to express his freedom.

That withstanding, how does a visual artist function?
During a collective live arts performance, designers, dancers and spectators are in a trance, together, in effervescence, transformed into a single flame. The artist draws what is happening between the dancers, and the dancers experiencing their adventure. Musicians improvise and dancers respond intuitively to the musicians' improvisation. The painter paints with his body.

The body makes decisions. We often say, for example, "I don't feel well, I'm leaving, I feel fine, I'm staying." We should therefore remember that consciousness is not one particular part of the brain and unconsciousness another. Consciousness and unconsciousness are two modes of functioning from the same area of the brain. Most of the time we function in unconscious mode and, in the wake of an alert, we go into conscious mode, in other words into a mode overexcited by the inundation of neurotransmissions emitted by the brain stem.

The conscious mode has this peculiarity of drawing on consciousness called nucleus, according to Damasio, made with deep first layers, called Registers of Consciousness, that connect Registers of the Object and Registers of Self, knowing that a large part of the functions (planning, memory etc.) also swing over to conscious mode, that is to say, they are overexcited by neurotransmitters, to give an extended consciousness.

3.3 Constant neuronal activity

When we are in conscious mode, it does not mean that certain areas of the brain, encapsulated as specialized areas of calculation, go on functioning in unconscious mode. These areas are wired from memorized experience, and fixed by genes, summoned up for the occasion.

Outside these areas, our grey matter is in perpetual movement, in inexhaustible combinatorics. It is this random activity which allows us to constantly construct scenarios and to anticipate situations, to create representations which belong to me only, to find a brilliant idea like Archimedes, and finally to ensure my freedom.

It often happens that we find an idea, which we are conscious of, but we don't know where it has come from. It's a question of the neuronal combinatorial effect, which works silently in unconscious mode.

3.4 The right and left brains
3.4.1 Betty Edwards' idea

Betty Edwards taught neuroscience applied to art at Long Beach University in California and published *Drawing with the Right Side of the Brain*.

She followed advances in neuroscience carefully and reported that two brains existed, the right and the left, which are in conflict when we observe the environment. She asked her students to draw

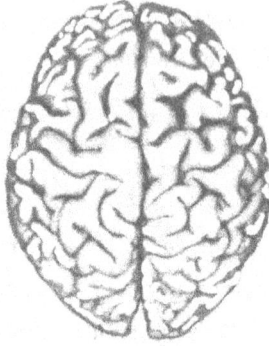

a portrait upside down to get them to see that the result was better than drawing the portrait the right way up. And yet it is difficult to know what we are drawing when the image is upside down. This experiment shows that the logical left brain is not only useless to the artist, but dangerous.

The right brain contains essentially relational and spatial functions. Its method of processing information is simultaneous, comprehensive, spatial and relational. It is from the sensitive world.

The left brain contains essentially nationality and language functions. Its method of processing information is linear, verbal, analytical and logical. It is from the rational, illusionary world.
Betty Edwards shows us how the left brain, mired in its rational culture, prevents the right brain from **seeing** the environment. She teaches her students to work with their right brain, and to **silence** their left brain. That is very far from the notion that considers language as the tool best adapted to managing our behaviour, and our perception of the world. Neuroscience also leads us to these conclusions.

I extend her defense of drawing as follows. Conceptual art does not require drawing abilities, and a lot of current artists consider this skill superfluous. However, it is rare to find students who feel sufficiently confident of their culture, their creative abilities, and their chances of success in the artistic world, to skip taking lessons.

To be successful in the conceptual art movement, without, in principle, superfluous effort, lazy young students run the risk of settling for a particular style, imitating models left by their elders who use repetitive figures serving as an identifiable signature for a clientele. They are then necrotized in a commercial prison.

I repeat the following main ideas to them.

1   Do not be afraid of trying to draw what will be for you a means of transfiguring the world.

2   Consider that this art enables you to discover, at each moment, what surrounds you, allowing you to develop your senses, your reflection of the world, concepts which allow you to understand the world, to go beyond it and to come back again.

3   Draw forth the essential, propose the strength of your
     sensibility and of your temperament. The words 'draw' and
     'design' have the same Latin origin, the words 'image'
     (*imago*, reproduction) and 'idea' (*eidos*, aspect, shape)
     express the same notion. Your drawing, your objective, is
     to try and understand and transfigure the world while
     developing your skills and your creativity.

4   Work every day, avoid letting your visual faculties and your
     means of expression, which will thus gain in strength,
     dwindle. Draw everything you see, you will be amazed at
     your discoveries and your ability to get to know the world.
     Picasso drew divinely. If he hadn't known how to draw, his
     paintings would have been dull.

*Tomorrow, if I wanted, I could get up, I could draw someone, I
could draw my mother from memory, I could do a strange abstract
painting. That's what I call freedom.*
                              – David Hockney.

3.4.2 Gazzaniga's experiment

So our brain comprises two principal and practically symmetrical
parts, one on the left and one on the right, separated by a deep
central groove. Whilst the left hemisphere is concerned with
speech, reasoning, and analysis, the right hemisphere is concerned
with meaning.

The coordination of the two hemispheres is apparently and
normally ensured by the corpus callosum, which is a connection
of neurons linking the two hemispheres. Gazzaniga shows us that
our left hemisphere can go on functioning without the right
hemisphere, resulting in quite surprising conclusions. It was in
attempting to treat epileptics that the phenomenon was first
identified. In the USA a few decades ago, epilepsy was treated by
disconnecting the left and the right hemispheres.

American surgeons severed the corpus callosum, which is composed of millions of neuronal axons that connect areas of the left hemisphere and the right hemisphere. Curious results ensued, both hemispheres demonstrating two distinct and independent cerebral activities. A patient having had such an operation is able to pick up and use a lighter with his left hand without being able to say what is in his left hand.

The right hemisphere, which controls the left hand, demonstrates awareness of the lighter, but the left hemisphere that holds the language centres, cannot name the object, as it has not received any information about the shape of the lighter from the right hemisphere.

This does not prevent the left hand, ordered by the right brain, from operating the lighter, that is to say, exchanging live information and energy with the environment.

Gazzaniga undertakes the following experiment in 1977. The patient is shown a screen. A message appears suddenly on the left-hand side of the screen, "Walk." The patient doesn't say anything but gets up and goes towards the door. Gazzaniga then asks his patient "Where are you going?" The patient replies "I'm going home to get a fruit juice."

In fact, only the right hemisphere, which contains the sensor-motorial areas, has seen the message in the left part of the field of vision without being able to transmit it to the left hemisphere.

The left hemisphere, which is the only one able to understand the word, ignores what the right brain, which triggered the walk, is doing. However. it understands that its body is in the process of walking towards the door.

So the left brain elaborates a fictitious conscious interpretation, "I'm going home to get a fruit juice", instead of saying: "I am leaving this room without knowing why." Without hesitating the patient imagined a fictitious scenario which justifies his position in the absence of information.

Yet, as healthy subjects, we are all like that. We are constantly imagining stories disconnected from reality. My son is late for our meeting: I envisage all sorts of hypotheses from the most ordinary to the most dramatic. In each situation multiple scenarios go round in our minds. An unrestrained combinatory is set in motion and my brain offers me thousands of fantastic scenarios, which I endeavour to control in the light of the few practical details that I possess.

We are constantly anticipating the evolution of our situation in order to adapt to circumstances and act. These anticipations are representations. These representations are not only fiction but also fantasy, and so abundant are they, that I may lack the ability to come down to Earth. I am lost in the world of belief.

Remarks on Part II
Our body changes
and our brain fantasizes

We imagine what we can't see and this imagined perception becomes a belief all the more unshakeable due to the fact that it doesn't have any opponents in the scope of imagination. Each of us, in fact, is free to imagine our world.

The scenario of the world that each person imagines depends on a chance combination of neurons in action. It would take the passing of generations and civilizations with their gods and fantasies to forget these beliefs.

We have observed that for its survival our body changes with its physical environment, whereas our brain imagines and fantasizes, whether or not it is connected to reality. This ability to fantasize has created dogmas such as Cartesianism, conceptual art or religious fantasies, which all have one point in common – to stifle life.

So, at this stage of our study, our perceptions are sources of illusion, and our representations result from our fantasies. Yet these are two ways of approaching physical reality, elusive to the physicist, but which, with every moment, our body interacts, in order to live.

This observation of the living being's exchanges with its physical environment contradicts Kant's vision, who saw an unattainable noumenon in the physical world.

Yet the phenomenon of vision, which only sees the world through its sensors, doesn't exclude the reality of the physical body, which goes on existing, even though in the west, from Plato to the German idealists, it has been rejected.

The living physical body can only exist in symbiosis and in constant exchange with its physical environment. Today we are having difficulties moving beyond twenty centuries of obscurantism and abstract idealism.

It is time to be unafraid of our body, to get to know it, to know how to live in it, rather than disregard or ignore it.

Today, enriched neuroscientific phenomenology, gives rise to the principle of three realities, which allow us to articulate approaches to pertinent problems, and to avoid confusion in defining notions, which are in fact polymorphous, with new approaches generating many discoveries.

PART III
We are the physical world

Introduction
Matter structures itself

We have seen that, contrary to Kant's idea, the physical world is perfectly tangible. Our body is in constant exchange with the physical world. At every instant that we breathe, and the oxygen that we absorb binds itself to the red blood cells which deliver the required amounts of energy to the muscles.

Solar radiation allows us to manufacture vitamin D. We ingest all sorts of elements that our organs are capable of dealing with – drawing on the sugar, fats, proteins and vitamins that it needs. In the course of Darwinian evolution our bodies have built sensors enabling the detection of positive or negative signals for our survival. Hence we are impoverished in the face of rapid technological advance, for example, when we breathe odourless carbon monoxide.

When it comes to our visual sensors, the dorsal pathway makes it possible to hit a tennis ball without making a mistake. It is the brain's ventral pathway of shapes and colours, which, by the illusions it generates, doesn't manage to grasp physical reality unambiguously. It is this construction cobbled-together by random Darwinian evolution that leads us to make errors of judgement in our environment.

Let us now remember briefly and simply two things:
-   Matter has structured itself to create the living being, that is what prebiotic chemistry teaches us,
-   On the scale of the living being symbiotic collaborations can be observed, that is what we see in biology, zoology and ethnology.

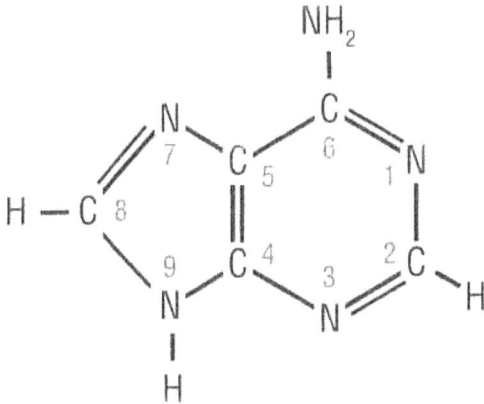

The organic compounds which make up the living being are a combination of mineral elements: carbon, oxygen, nitrogen and hydrogen. This here is the character of Adenine, one of the basic components of the DNA, which carries our genetic signature. Stanley Miller produced this substance very simply in 1953 with an electric arc, in other words lightning, applied to a soup of hydrogenated mineral substances.

Chapter 1
We are stardust

The physical mineral world is organized by supplying itself with the first organic elements of prebiotic chemistry. In the laboratory we have recently reconstructed this phase of the birth of a living being.

If we situate ourselves on a larger scale, that of the living being, we can observe that we not only live in constant exchange with the mineral environment, but also with the living being, particularly when we thrive on symbiotic exchanges.

1.1   Stanley Miller and John Sutherland

In Chicago in 1953, Stanley Miller reconstructed an atmosphere of hydrogenated substances, which he submitted to electric discharges, which on Earth we call lightning. This atmosphere represented the original soup that surrounded our nascent planet. After a week Miller discovered in his jar, pieces of the basics of organic chemistry, in other words living chemistry: amino acids, water, formaldehyde, ribose, hydrocyanic acid, adrenalin.

Many experiments took place bringing about other amino acids, pyrimidines, purines and sugars.

In 2007 John Sutherland, Matthew Powner and Béatrice Gerland from Manchester University, England, succeeded in synthesizing, in the absence of proteins, two out of the four nitrogenous bases of the RNA molecule that carries genetic information.

Their idea was to make a prebiotic energy soup in a random fashion in the form of an electric arc, while respecting the diurnal and nocturnal frequency specific to the Earth.

1.2 The living being exchanges constantly with the outside world

The living being must maintain its inner balance. This can only be done in a dynamic way, depending on variations in the environment. In order to do that a cell opens and closes its doors as much as is needed. Every animal absorbs the environment and throws back its waste products after having drawn on the consumed energy. Thus the living being exports its internal disorder and can only live and develop within its ecosystem.

According to Heidegger, as a philosopher, we are the being thrown into the world we are the being here, present in the world, here and now. But we are also part of the world, we are not only *"here"* but also *"the here and now."*

1.3 The emergence of the mind

Emergence is a phenomenon which amazes us but which is common, right from very elementary levels. Chlorine and sodium are very aggressive but table salt is essential to life. Oxygen burns us, hydrogen is dangerous, but water is the basis of our organic construction. Lightning coming from clouds has created life. Defense or attack behaviour emerges from a group of bacteria. Likewise, for a symphonic orchestra, the activity specific to an orchestral system, composed of subsystems of musicians, generate the life of the music, unique and ephemeral purpose, which produces an emotion in me. The specific activity of a system generates its behaviour - in other words, the life we perceive. Our mind emerges from our cerebral and corporal neuron activity. We have defined thought as a group of cerebral activities, which express themselves in decision, planning, perception, representation, and which can take place consciously or unconsciously.

The alterity of the other is the neuronal image of the other dealt with by my thought.

Chapter 2
The living being is symbiotic

Plant and animal cells have a nucleus. They also contain organelles, like mitochondria and plastids, whose ancestors were bacteria. These bacteria live in perfect positive collaboration with their host. Such symbiotic associations can be observed on a corporal scale or in animal communities.

1.1 The nucleus cell, a shared house

Eukaryotic cells are living beings equipped with a nucleus. They can be either unicellular (amoeba, paramecium, etc.) in general larger than 10 to 100 micron bacteria, or pluricellular organisms: mushrooms, plants, invertebrates and vertebrates.

The eukaryotic cell contains specialized compartments and organelles: the nucleus containing genetic material, the mitochondria containing enzymes necessary for the cell to breathe, plastids containing the enzymes, and plastids necessary for plant and algae photosynthesis, ribosomes containing the RNA necessary for protein synthesis.

However, if eukaryotic cell organelles had appeared progressively, intermediate forms should be found. Yet this is not the case. Lynn Margulis has concluded that we are in the presence of ancient bacteria, living symbiotically within a larger cell, based on the following observations. Mitochondria and plastids have similar dimensions to bacteria. Moreover, these organelles contain DNA, RNA messengers, ribosomes and transfer RNA, which enable them to multiply independently from the nucleus cell, and to synthesize certain proteins with their own genes.

This would indicate that these organelles were formerly able to self-reproduce and to synthesize all their proteins. These organelles could have had bacteria as ancestors that originally lived independently. They would then have become permanent hosts of large bacteria, and thus symbiosis would have been established between the different partners, which were the first eukaryotic unicellular beings.

1.2   The ecosystem inseparable from the living being

What is symbiosis? It is concerned with the association of two sorts of living beings, each finding an advantage in this association. Symbiosis is a win-win partnership between two living beings.

The case most often quoted is that of the hermit crab, a crustacean living inside an abandoned shell, and a sort of sea anemone which attaches itself to the outside of the shell. The anemone protects the hermit crab by means of its stinging tentacles and, in return, takes advantage of the crustacean's food waste.

Similarly, the *Paramecium bursaria* hosts green unicellular algae of the type *Chlorella3*. This very mobile ciliated organism, lives on the surface of fresh water, seeks habitats well-lit by the sun: the algae thrives on this exposure and so produces, by photosynthesis, a maximum of substances on which the paramecium feeds.

Intestinal flora is a good example of mutualism, in other words cooperation between different kinds of organisms involving an advantage for each.

Organisms in symbiosis have acquired metabolic particularities, which they don't have in a separate state: the association is transmitted from generation to generation. We also know of associations such as the pilot or suction fish, which take advantage of a shark to travel.

Another phenomenon is the living being's adjustment to the ecosystem. One example is the perfect adaptation of rice to Asian countries and the fact that Asians possess an enzyme to digest rice that western people don't have.

1.3 Husserl and the impossible balance without the environment

A living cell, like all other living beings, is in constant exchange with its environment. It opens and closes its doors according to its needs, in order to function, develop and reproduce.

Removing a cell's environment amounts to the same as killing the cell. In certain cases, to survive, bacteria form spores or adopt a vegetative way of life when the environment becomes hostile, which means, in this case, that the environment, although hostile, still exists. The bacteria will go back to their exchanges when outside conditions improve.

Yet this hypothesis of the removal of a being's environment that Husserl puts forward in his *"Cartesian meditations"* where he claims that the alterity of the other is a "pure self" which needs nothing to survive. According to him, the Other would exist without anyone having identified him. This idea is in fact conceivable in an abstract Platonist inspired philosophy, but doesn't make sense on our Earth.

We should be wary of transcendental intuitions which are used as representations of the world, in this case of a world which doesn't exist, that don't take physical and perceived realities into consideration.

In fact, we know that biologically the Other can only live in society, in relation to the environment and other living beings, that a muscle cell lives in a muscle, that legionella or staphylo bacteria know how to group together, and so recognize each other, that they only develop certain proteins in a group, which will allow them to survive in case of an attack.

Remarks on Part III
A composite brain

We have difficulties in understanding the physical world, most probably because of the insufficient quality of our measuring instruments, but especially due to the fact that we always have presuppositions about things we observe even before observing them.

Our body, for its part, without taking into consideration the logical brain, knows what its physical needs are, expresses itself and acts as a consequence to ensure its survival.

Kant (1724-1804) wanted to develop what he called reason, in other words the ability to know, to judge and to act in compliance with social norms, while leaving a part to belief, to make possible, according to him, morality and hope.

This dividing line between reason and belief was beneficial to the development of Descartes' rationalism and modern scientific thought. Yet this dividing line has also been disastrous, in so far as it ignored the body, and in that way, lead modern man to human and societal impasses.

Heidegger's (1889-1976) philosophy thus seemed like a return to Earth, when he invites us to live here, to be this world.

Part IV
The three realities here and now

Introduction
Pirandello's (1867-1936)
doubt

In 1929 Pirandello produced a strange drama for theatre called "*As you want me.*" A woman absent for twenty years comes back and claims to be her husband's wife. The husband recognizes her but his friends are puzzled. The latter don't really recognize her and manage to plant doubt in the husband's mind. A kind of police inquest develops. Finally, after arguments about travel memories or material proof like beauty spots, the wife says to her husband "No matter, I am as you want me."

No matter in fact the physical reality, or that he is no longer able to remember her "beauty spots" or distinguishing marks; no matter the perceived reality, as today she is no longer to him the one who made him dream, no matter how he pictured her, as the idea he had of his wife has been modified over time.

The husband is faced with a new woman whose materiality, the reactions she provokes in him, and his idea about her, have become divorced. He could have his wife back if one of the three approaches, physical, perceived or imagined, had been successful.

We can already understand that these three realities depend on a place and a time.

The choice of a point of view

I was with a friend in a stuffy bourgeois restaurant and I was familiar with his political opinions. We were glad to see each other, and to begin with we had ordered drinks; for him a "*berrichon*" - a red Menetou wine with raspberry cordial, and for me a "*communard*" in other words - a red Menetou wine with blackcurrant cordial. A few minutes later a waiter dressed in a tuxedo came up to us ceremoniously with the two awaited drinks on his tray and announces " A *berrichon* and a *cardinal*!" Thus my communard had been transformed into a cardinal! I wondered if such a thing would be drinkable. However, it was indeed a Menetou with blackcurrant cordial.

Doubtlessly the poetic fantasy evoked by the communard concept was not the same in both cultures, mine and the owner of the bourgeois restaurant. This little adventure sums up perhaps three hundred pages of an essay entitled "*What is philosophy?*" in which Deleuze and Guattari expound the truism, according to which, a concept is only valid in relation to a conceptual plan, that we can understand as a cultural landscape, which is only accessible at a given point in time, only as a point of view.

The analysis must not be forgotten when reading the following exercises. The three realities proposed for each of the concepts approached, refer anyhow to our era, and to varying cultural contexts. Therefore the reader should not consider the following forms as an explanation of things, but as an invitation to get involved in a multiple, and rich approach to the world, in order to avoid misunderstandings with oneself, and others. Those who sail have learned how to triangulate their position along the ocean's coasts. Nothing is ever certain, but probable, and it is a plural and diversified view, which enables us to understand things.

In this fourth part we will study the nature of the three realities through examples of current everyday life. We will then attempt to draw general lines specific to each of these realities.

Chapter 1
Real and everyday examples of the three realities

1.1 Trade negotiation:
How to concretize a business

What does concrete mean?

Let us remember that realizing something concrete proves intelligence. Concrete doesn't mean simple. In trade we seek to create a lasting exchange of goods and services against cash flow. Intelligence takes multiple factors into consideration.

We negotiate ceaselessly every day. Will my negotiation at the present time end in failure, or success, in a Pyrrhic victory, or a win-win result? If I want to maintain stable commercial relationships (chosen point of view), I adopt a win-win negotiation objective.

A successful negotiation should take into consideration three approaches to reality from the client's point of view.

Represented: What he says, how he sees the world

Perceived: What he feels, how he functions

Physical: What I should know, pure and simple, concrete facts that I must be familiar with.

In other words, I must not only take into consideration the partnership, its history and its psychology, but also the dynamic environment which serves as a framework and backdrop to this negotiation. In fact, it seems quite natural, as a matter of fact, to remain realistic and to take into consideration the multiple factors, which contribute to the creation and upkeep of stable and lasting relationships.

The shopkeeper's point of view represented in this graphic. They must be able to move around their customer's three realities, mentally to get them to converge towards action. Commercial action consists of finding common ground, communicating terms and making a positive exchange for both partners.

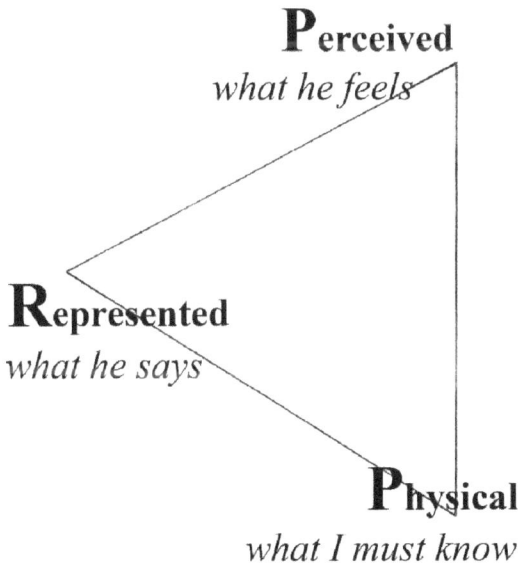

Perceived
what he feels

Represented
what he says

Physical
what I must know

1.2 A coin

Physically a coin is a round piece of metal, more or less decorated, **perceived** as purchasing power at the baker's, but also as the impression of consuming its destiny or the impression of manipulating its world.

It is **represented** in drawing by a circle, if it is seen face on, a right-hand segment, if it is seen in profile, an ellipse, if it is seen at an angle.

The point of view is a common man's.

Yet if we take the numismatist point of view, a coin is **physically** a piece of metal, **perceived** as an object of great historical value, revealing changes in perhaps unexpected places and **represented** by suitable terms closer to representations or ancient texts.

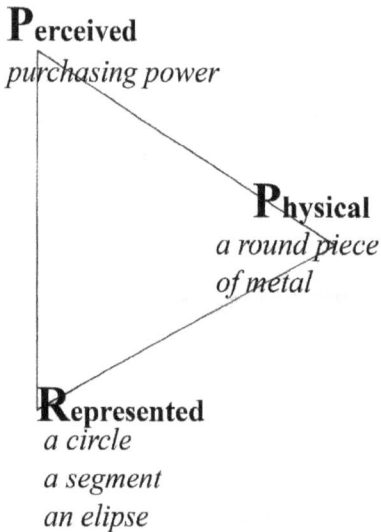

Perceived
purchasing power

Physical
*a round piece
of metal*

Represented
*a circle
a segment
an elipse*

1.3   The Sun: why light is neutral

We **perceive** the Sun as a source of light and heat. The Egyptians **represented** it as the god Ra wearing a falcon's head on top of the solar disc. Yet **physically** it is a star, in other words a vast viscous mass of fusioning matter which splutters energy out in all directions in the form of lava, and of alpha, beta and gamma nuclear radiation.

The Sun is indifferent about sending its rays into the cosmos, it emits energy haphazardly, without any purpose. That is why the artist, who is nowadays familiar with quantum mechanical laws of chance, considers that light is "neutral". When painting, it gives the qualifiers which correspond to his perception, according to his needs, relating to the desired effects: the light will be soft, harsh, charged, pale, fresh, penetrating, to bring a charged, joyful, sidereal, burning or freezing atmosphere.

This point of view breaks down the barriers to knowledge.

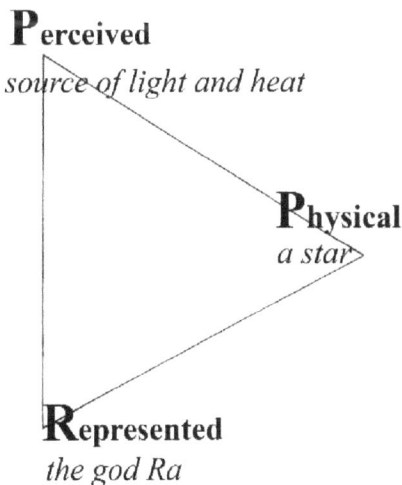

Perceived
source of light and heat

Physical
a star

Represented
the god Ra

1.4 Visible light and colour

According to experiment, light is **physically**, either solar energy propagated in a straight line, a periodic wave, or a shower of energy seeds. In theory it is an electromagnetic wave. Visible light is a group of frequencies in the range of visible frequencies. One particular frequency corresponds to one colour.

Colour is **perceived** as the quality of an object and the light received, or through a glass filter, as a rainbow, or in listening to a Geiger counter, as the little showers that make the loud speaker crackle.

It is **represented** by classical painters with areas of light colours contrasting with dark areas, namely by pigments. Yet we know that historically, colour has changed meaning, in the Middle Ages blue was a warm colour.

This point of view is modern.

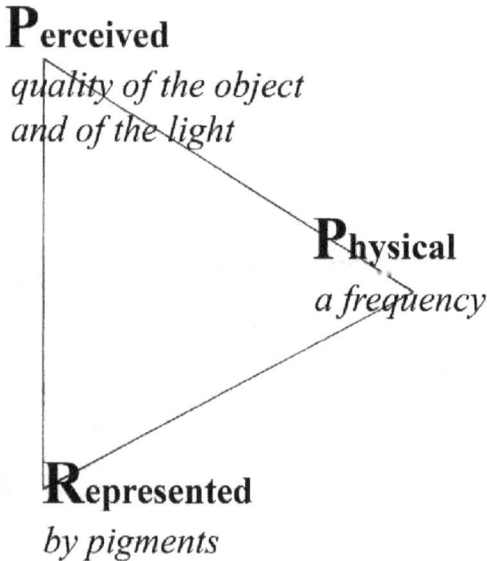

Perceived
*quality of the object
and of the light*

Physical
a frequency

Represented
by pigments

1.5 Performing a tango: the past present and the future present

Physically we are in the present.

The tribe has fixed a time and date for a rendezvous, which has now arrived. The tango is a popular dance, namely, an affective and collective moment with one's tribe.

Social conventions are to be adhered to, otherwise the group of dancers would make no sense at all, and the aesthetic would disappear. The music sets the tone, gives the rhythm or pace, even if an infinity of steps and figures, are possible within each moment.

On his canvas, the painter grasps elements of each instant of time unfolding. The present, as a physical entity, does not reveal itself completely; we can only perceive a tiny, ephemeral part. Grasping the present as if it were a question of eternity or totality, would only be a vision of death.

Perception is the immediate future.

The dancer decides, that is to say, he anticipates, leads the action, he is in the future. The two dancers are sternum to sternum, she indicates what she wants her dance partner to do by her torso, or by the position of her feet on the ground.

Thus the dancers can constantly improvise to the music. The music, whether improvised or not, is, for the group of dancers, a source interpreted in movements specific to each of them. Noëlle told me *"Michel must pay attention to five things: to the figure he is making, to the figure which is going to take place, to the reactions of his partner who is following him or who is going to follow him or who is going to ask him to perform a figure, to the obstacles which he is about to encounter, and of course the music.*

In order to do that, like Alice, he has to go to the other side of the mirror. In an autohypnotic state, we can feel all sorts of sensations and we perform the movements that we have to."

The representation of a tango performance relates the past
The dancer becomes observer. The observer reconstructs the scene which is taking place or that he imagines from past experience. The observer is in the past with all his memory mobilized.

His episodic memory relates the past history of a happy moment, movements, smells, music, lightness of the body, mind intensity, the impression of filling up the dance hall, the melody which carries the couple along.

I can also attempt to relive the past, organize a new dance session, represent myself in the future which would be a new dance session, but I know that nothing will be like it was before and that forming an idea of the future is only my excessiveness in wanting to fight against chance. The future I will live in will never resemble the future that I have imagined.

The point of view is the dancers'.

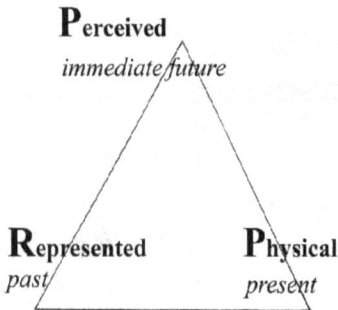

Perceived
immediate future

Represented   **P**hysical
past   *present*

1.6 Time

What can we say then about time, which only passes in one single direction?

If truth be told, after years studying and teaching physics I dont really know what time is, any more than I can explain the arrow of time. That doesn't prevent us from covering pages in equations taking into account that variable which allowed Aristotle to explain movement.

For Bergson and Husserl **perceived** time is a psychological duration. Time has been **represented** since the appearance of the first instruments conceived for measuring it such as sundials and water-clocks.

Mathematical and mechanical time is a representation by Greek mathematicians who treated it as one of the dimensions of space. Western time is rectilinear and goes past regularly. Hindu time is cylindrical in an eternal recurrence.

The point of view is a researcher's lost in the Underworld.

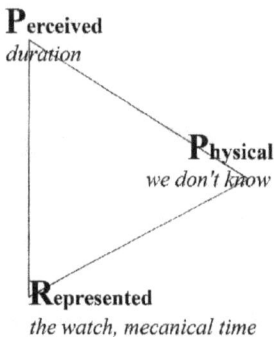

Perceived
duration

Physical
we don't know

Represented
the watch, mecanical time

1.7 Music

What happens in music?

For the physicist and physician Helmholtz, it concerns vibration. It is **perceived** as a source of emotions for musicians, for those who listen and those who dance to the sound of music.

It is also perceived as a direct source of knowledge, to communication with the world. Yet if I listen to traditional Chinese music, I don't understand anything, my impression of access to the truth is seriously dented.

Composers **represent** it as a musical score with a mechanical aspect, a transmitter of emotion that is not by any means mechanical.

The point of view is a researcher's who must successively endorse the culture of each participant cited: physician, musician, and composer. Each culture corresponds to a conceptual world, yet also to an individual or collective sensitive memory.

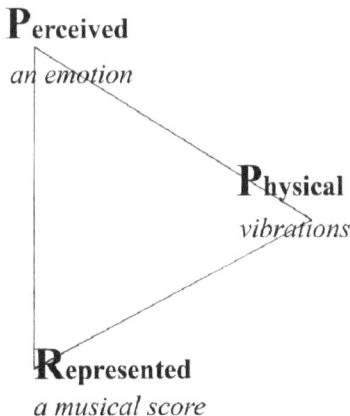

Perceived
an emotion

Physical
vibrations

Represented
a musical score

1.8 Architectural verticality, the curved pillars experiment

In 1909 Robert Delaunay visited the Saint Séverin church in the fifth arrondissement in Paris and has left us a number of drawings and lithographs of the Ambulatory. The uninformed reader may attribute the curve of the pillars to an artist's fantasy. Going there, you will notice that Delaunay did in fact see curved pillars. More astonishing you will see curved pillars in Bourges and in all Cathedrals, but you will also see curved walls in the streets of New York or San Francisco.

©LM Services BV© photo CNAC/MNAM
Dist RMN©Philippe Migeat

Why then don't we **perceive** the straight pillars as they were physically built by the stone masons? Because we have two spherical eyes which offer us a perception in a visual cylindrical universe.

The plan which is formed by a straight pillar and our eyes which are practically at the same point in space cut the cylinder following an ellipse.

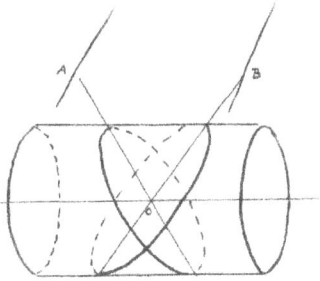

Thus we see an ellipse in three-dimensional space. Yet when what is seen in three-dimensional space has to be **represented** on a sheet of paper, which is a two-dimensional space, the visual cylinder has to be unfolded (and not projected) onto the sheet of paper.

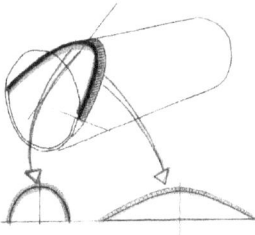

The unfolding of the cylinder skin (let's imagine a sausage) onto the sheet of paper gives a trigonometric curve. The mathematical demonstration is given in my book *Drawing in Real Perspective*. **The point of view**, making a multiple approach possible, is of the artistic designer and mathematician, sensitive to different aesthetics.

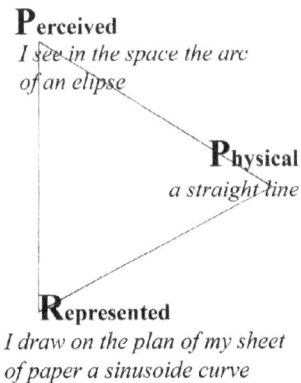

Perceived
*I see in the space the arc
of an elipse*

Physical
a straight line

Represented
*I draw on the plan of my sheet
of paper a sinusoide curve*

1.9 Death, the passage to non-being

The three western realities seem to be the following:

Physically this concerns the passage to non-being, the homeostatic balance being broken.

Its **perception** corresponds to a sudden collapse, due to the activation of a somatic marker, at the thought of the representation of a death experience. Indeed, according to Seneca (4 BCE-65 CE), *It is not that we have a short time to live, but that we waste a lot of it, through not accepting, that it will one day come to an end.* This moment is represented in many ways depending on the civilizations and cultures of an era. So many people, so many fantasies. In ancient Egypt the deceased could live with its mummy, which is however only the appearance of a body. For Hindus, the spirit is reincarnated in another body. To the Buddha, the infernal reincarnation cycle ends in enlightenment. In Greek antiquity, Paradise doesn't exist, it was neither produced by the oracles, nor promised by the priests. For Homer (circa 8th century BCE), lost souls wander in the underworld, the kingdom of Hades.

For Democritus (460-370 BCE) atoms belong to the cosmos. For Plato (428-348 BCE) dying makes access to the Truth possible. In current Christian interpretations, the soul of the dead contemplates the face of God, no longer thinks, and lives an instant of eternal ecstasy. For the scientist, the hydrogen cycle pursues its course.

The point of view is of common mortals.

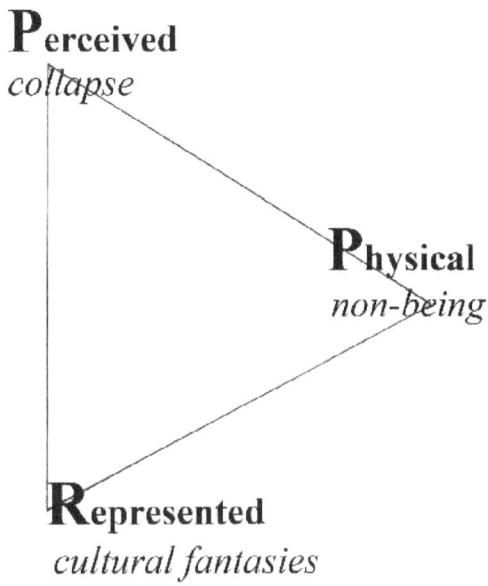

Perceived
collapse

Physical
non-being

Represented
cultural fantasies

1.10. The unclear truth of the court

The point of view is the person subject to trial

The physical reality is an action, which is over.

The perceived reality is the inner conviction of the jury members in the case of a crown court, or the judges in other cases. The action is still present in the prosecutor's memory, like a lingering stain that must be wiped clean by society.

The represented realities are facts reconstructed by witness statements, consistency of revealed clues, previous history, ensuing sanctions, indicating the seriousness of deeds.

A verdict is then returned taking into account those elements, which may not very substantial. The action is over. Inner conviction is subjective. The pieces, the clues and testimonies give rise to hypotheses, deductions, contestation, imagined scenarios, requiring means, money and time.

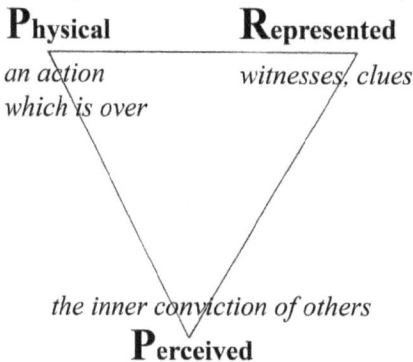

Physical   **R**epresented

an action   *witnesses, clues*
which is over

the inner conviction of others
Perceived

1.11 The Christian Saint Trinity

The Romans distinguished between *spiritus*, the spirit which reasons, and *animus* the soul in its animality.

How can the source of the spirit be represented for those who refuse to see its origin in matter? The Christians imagined, instead of a **physical** source, a transcendent one, namely God the father. The father is **represented** by the word of Christ, bearer of his message. And so that this message could be **perceived**, a catalyst had to be called upon, the Holy Spirit, who gets the apostles to understand the message, while making them speak in tongues, if not to leave their world, at least to go towards others, to convince them.

The **point of view** is a spiritualist one. The biblical narrative seems to have its origin in Egyptian mythology. The dogma of the Holy Spirit, as an entity, has taken form historically, by progressively giving the Spirit the same rank as the Son and the Father. The Spirit is a totally disembodied conception, autonomous, but hosting the Son as well as the Father.

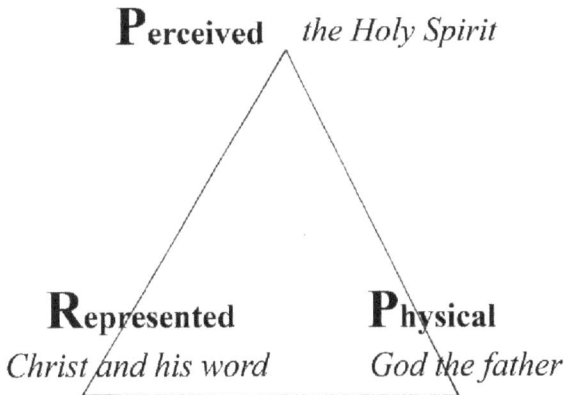

Perceived   *the Holy Spirit*

Represented   **P**hysical
Christ and his word   *God the father*

1.12 Bacteria

We are living in a time of reversal similar to the Renaissance, and every day we discover new challenges. Let us stop and look at one of them which casts doubt on our anthropocentric vision of things. Consider the social behaviour of bacteria, which have, unlike man, neither neurons, a nervous system, nor a brain.

Some bacteria have a pertinent and ingenious behaviours of defense and attack, individually or in a group. They recognize each other, in groups they develop proteins, which they never develop on their own. This allows them to ensure the protection of the colony with a biofilm. They also have a social organization in their survival strategy, they inject their healthy DNA into a sibling, sick from an antibiotic attack.

This phenomenon tests us, and shows us that whilst we can find a material explanation for our behaviour, such as we have presented above, we have difficulty interpreting bacterian behaviour with these anthropological notions, because we willingly imagine, and wrongly so, that everything is in our image.

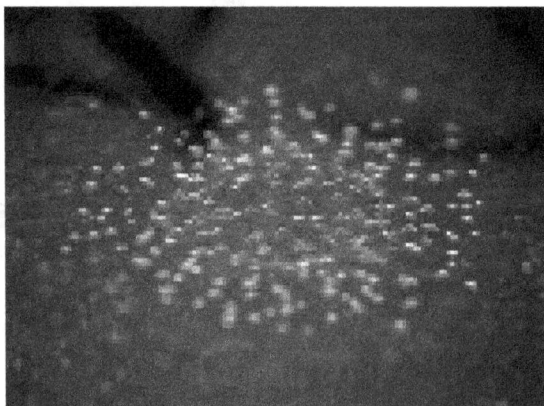

Mycococcus xanthus come together, implying that they know how to situate themselves and recognize each other.

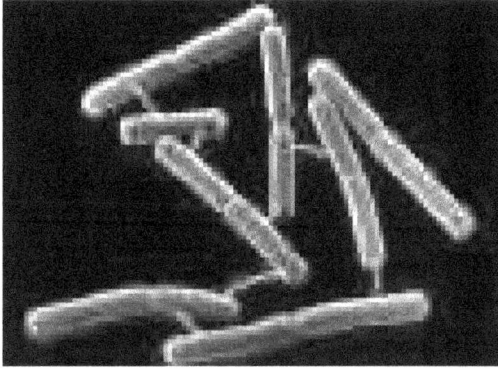

Bacillus subtilis communicating by Nanotubes

The point of view is a researcher's who takes the three realities into consideration.

Physically a bacterium is a living element responding to the same laws, in other words, chance, thermodynamics, genetics and epigenetics.

We **Perceive** behaviour.

Our **Representation** of this behaviour is an anthropomorphism. We distinguish the "good" and "bad" bacteria, we are surprised at their attack and defense strategies, without admitting nevertheless that these living beings could have a mind.

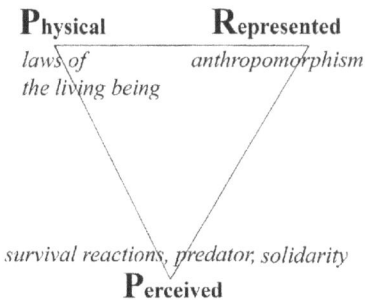

Physical   **R**epresented
laws of   *anthropomorphism*
the living being

survival reactions, predator, solidarity
Perceived

Chapter 2
The nature of the three realities

1.1 Perceived reality

In the first part we have seen that the images of reality that we create are not photographs. For vision we have seen that 80% of the fibres that come into the optical area don't come from the eye. Our sensors help us to act in order to survive, and not to take photos. *Perception prepares for action.*

Perception is a complex processing of information coming from the whole body. My destabilized inner balance is my body's emotion. My perception is active according to my intended action, my memory, my anticipations, my multi-sensorial information, and my body's reactions. We have seen that different parts of the body give different kinds of information not always synchronous, but which enables our body to make immediate, pertinent, and unconscious action despite our erroneous perception. Perceived reality is firstly a corporal or mental illusion, which doesn't describe physical reality with precision and certainty.

1.2 Represented reality

In the second part we have seen that represented reality is the result of our unconscious and random neuronal activity, such as it appears in neuroscience. The unlikely and unexpected scenarios which result constitute our fantasies which, confronted with registered schemas, may eventually, though rarely, provoke the cry *"Eureka!"*.

Lionel Naccache reminds us that the fiction, which enables me to ceaselessly reconstruct the world, is the source of my freedom. Alain Berthoz underlines that in constantly reconstructing the world, I will find scenarios which will enable me to anticipate and act.

For Michel Foucault, when at a societal level, the emphasis is on the influence of intended action on thought, the representation becomes the expression of power, reconstructing the historical narrative in one's interests. For Jacques Derrida, the fabrication of represented reality is, in other words, the determining logos of good and bad.

1.3 Physical reality

Physical reality is intermediate, unpredictable, and implacable. It has an autonomous life determined by chance.

Physical reality can only be perceived through our senses and our measuring instruments, which interpose each other. For Kant, it was directly inaccessible for this very reason.

Physical reality presented in this way is evasive and contains something paradoxical, since its essence is, first of all, to be tangible. We are part of it, from which interminable misunder-standings, like Schrödinger's dead or alive cat, with which he wants to illustrate quantum mechanics. In fact, in this allegory is Schrödinger talking about perceived reality, or indeed physical reality. The famous cat is described in Annex 2.

Thus in our rational world a dereliction appears, an incomplete logic. The physical world inherently tangible, can only be approached via the illusions of our perception, or represented by our fantasies. Yet it is our *logos*, which leads us to such an absurdity, because this logos is not the physical world.

The paramecium, which doesn't have a brain, constantly exchanges, grows and multiplies in symbiosis with its physical environment, with which it opens and closes its doors according to its needs.

We have seen, that in the physical world, and we can notice it at each instant, that physical reality is far from being inaccessible. We live in a physical reality, interacting with it every second. My body needs air, sun, food. Physical reality is ourselves immersed in our environment.

1.4   The autonomy of the three realities

Each of the three realities evolves at its own speed. Perceived reality, in the presence of an object, is a function of physical reality, of memory, intended action, corporal and physical needs.

Represented reality, in the absence of the object, is another function of physical reality, of memory, intended action, corporal and physical needs.

Each of these two realities, *perceived* and *represented*, are not of the same nature, don't correspond to the same needs, are not elaborated by the same parts of our body. Represented reality corresponds to the left brain and perceived reality to the right.

The two realities, perceived and represented, don't evolve at the same speed. As for the physical world, it has a life of its own; it is born, it lives, and it dies.

Each of these worlds, physical, perceived and represented, is therefore autonomous, each having its own ephemeral existence, even if links exist between them. Thus the Sun progressively reduces and will inevitably become a black hole.

Our perception of heat depends on individuals and circumstances. Moses, bearer of light, was in the Renaissance represented with horns by Michaelangelo. The God of Moses wasn't identified by physics, but he was perceived by mystics in their stigmatas and represented in the form of an old man with a long white beard. The perceptions were numerous and evolutionary.

1.5 Links between the three realities

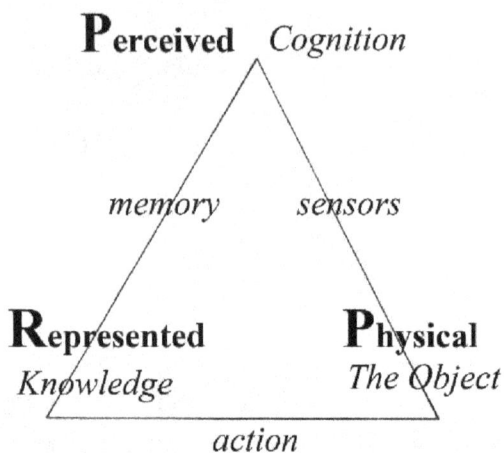

Perceived *Cognition*

memory   *sensors*

Represented   **P**hysical
Knowledge   *The Object*

action

Our sensors collect information from our environment, in particular, from an object we're interested in. The sensors we possess are of varying quality. In the ear a single membrane vibrates. The first telephone lines carried information with 24 bauds, today very high-speed lines actually transport thousands of low speed conversations.

Images require a very large quantity of information. The back of the eye contains a considerable number of sensors (rods and cones), which capture the image on the matrix that they form.

Perception uses the sensors of the five senses (sight, hearing, smell, touch, taste) but also muscular and articular, proprioceptive sensors, such as the internal ear, pressure sensors, tension, oxygen, as well as internal information such as intended action, decision, and memory.

Representation uses memory and focuses on the action.

Remarks on Part IV
Jean Baudrillard and reality

Jean Baudrillard (1929-2007) makes the point that the reality we have in front of us doesn't interest anyone. He tells us "How therefore does our desire bear on the object?" or indeed "Our relationship with reality is exuberant." According to him the true object is absent. Each of us evokes reality in our own way.

Jean Baudrillard concludes that the world is not adapted to our desires, yet, in saying that, he forgets that the world is purposeless. The living being is born aimlessly and the world doesn't care about their desires, especially when these are really needs necessary to its survival and growth.

Above we have seen that in order to develop, the ever off balance being can only grow by exporting its entropy into the environment. Thus, by its nature, the being is first of all a predator.

Our desire will always bear on the missing object like romantic passion, but this desire, this need, this "I love you" "Je t'aime" "Te quiero "Je te veux" "I want you, I need you" in my view, is only the expression of the nature of our living being, that is to say, our predatory nature.

In this way Eros, the vital spark, and Phileo, the love which Agape gives and receives, would be love which is unrequited but which needs resources in order to give. In all cases, energy transfer exists, the living being gathers strength and develops through the Other, and in the environment.

It must also be noted that our brain can only understand the perceived world by drawing on several senses. Therefore, the loss of balance can give me the impression that the floor of my bedroom has become the ceiling, requiring the reorganization of my brain. Our perception is and can only be multi-sensorial.

The left brain calculates and compares, the right brain perceives. The registers of consciousness take my inner perceptions from my Self and outer perceptions from the Object, into consideration. My Self and the Other, in other words, from my material and social environment.

Hip Hop street dancer 2- 24.04.2013. Thumbnail sketch.
Felt tip pen on ordinary white A4 80g paper. Xavier Bolot. This drawing is neither a photo nor a series of stills.

PART V
Realities
and societies
in evolution

Introduction
People's beliefs

People are born and die with their beliefs. Bergson ponders: how can we relate the truth that we are part of? Habit makes living without thinking possible, but everything shifts. We can now see that if three realities are necessary to approach the Other, these three realities will evolve over time, change weight, which will, unknowingly, change the values of a society in the course of its history.

We haven't become accustomed to the truth, indeed it is a source of disquiet, we prefer our representation to be disconnected from the reality that we want long term.

We have invented the concept of truth because it brought us the comfort of stability, a planned pathway, laziness, egotism, and the worst injustices. In fact, at one point, in one particular place, the strongest reason is always the best. Imposed truth is the dominant individual's; whether or not this reason corresponds to the logic admitted by society or a reality of knowledge.

The best reasons will be those which give the living being the advantage and the possibility to exert its predatory nature. In this context, all reasons that explain the world in its way, to survive, will be right.

Patrick Verstichel and Lionel Naccache insist on this point. In neurology we can observe, concerning Gazzaniga's experiment, that we have a particularly obstinate left brain. The narrative left brain makes up a story and sticks to it. Therefore, the truth, the result of rejected realities, will evolve in our minds and mutate in the course of social reversals.

Nevertheless, in order to expose each era's predominant values, we are going to attempt to discern three realities, which enable us to articulate causes of evolution, and observed mutations more clearly.

Here it is not a question of establishing an exhaustive picture but recognizing a few markers, as reflections on our social evolution.

We will examine the three realities practiced in the evolution of western societies by describing a few highlights.

- Premodernity
- Modernity
- Postmodern reaction

Conceptual upheavals and priorities will appear naturally.

Chapter 1
Premodernity

Homer explained that we must live in harmony with the world, that is to say, with the Cosmos and the Gods, and that our hubris, in other words the excess of our passions and pride, is the source of misfortunes. Greek polytheism is based on fundamental laws of being: man is finite, ephemeral, conscious of his death, and can understand himself.

Ever since, ancient philosophy has been composed of multiple bubbling currents. Philosophers succeed one another, each taking the opposite view from his predecessor, which is still the case today. We are accustomed to opposing, rightly so, Democritus and Plato, but forget to mention their common points. What realities then will the young Aristotle, who is going to inspire our Middle Ages, propose?

1.1 Democritus of Abdera (460 - 370)

The Son of a dignitary, he was thirty years older than Plato. Democritus spent his fortune making a number of journeys, learning geometry in Egypt and astronomy in Persia.

He laughed at men who apply themselves to searching for imaginary goods, or indeed who make projects requiring several lives of them. He had a simple life because he affirmed that he who knows how to enjoy himself with little is always quite rich. He accepted everyone in his company without social consideration.

In his observations, he repudiates mythological notions and

THE THREE REALITIES ᐊ 105

explains natural phenomena by experimentation and observation of nature. We are indebted to him for the first systematic formulation of the atomic theory, which he derived from the following reasoning:

If anybody is infinitely divisible, this would suggest two things either nothing will remain or something will remain. In the first case, matter would have a virtual existence, in the second case we ask the question: What remains? The answer is more logical, it is the existence of real elements, indivisible and unbreakable called *atoms*, meaning "can't be divided."

Democritus deduced the following consequences. In nature there are only atoms and emptiness, which are at the origin of all compounds whether they be the Sun or indeed the soul, which is made up of air. Atoms move around eternally in infinite emptiness. They collide and rebound at random and join up according to their shape, but they never become mixed up. It is under the action of atoms and emptiness that things expand and disintegrate. Visible things and everything that is perceptible by the senses is composed of corpuscles. The being is therefore not one, but composed of corpuscles. Note that Democritus' intuition, which he had obtained from Anaxagoras (500-428 BCE) was confirmed by the chemist Lavoisier (1743-1794) who concluded "Nothing gets lost, nothing is created, everything transforms"

For Democritus, the soul dies with the body.

Sensitive qualities are the conventions determined by our opinions and our affections. We aren't aware of all our sensations: a large number of them remain unnoticed. Sense impressions vary according to animals, from one individual to another, and even within an single individual.

It is impossible to know which impressions are real, they are all equally real. Everything that appears to an individual and that seems to exist, is real. In other words, my perception is my reality. "In reality we don't know anything, because truth is at the bottom of the well." Democritus distinguishes between two forms of knowledge: knowledge of the senses, according to him slanted and obscure, and knowledge by intellect, which he calls legitimate and true. Reason is the criteria of legitimate knowledge.

Democritus had a number of enemies. Plato took an opposing view wanted to burn his writings, in the same way as the religious institutions, whose business assets prosper in the notion of immortality of the soul and who exploit the terror of the beyond. The Christians will therefore discredit this materialistic philosophy, relentlessly burning his writings and his philosophies, in the same way that Muslims burned, at the time of their conquests, the Persian libraries in 630 and the Alexandria libraries in 642, or else the Afghan Taliban who bombarded the Buddhas of Bâmiyân in 2001.

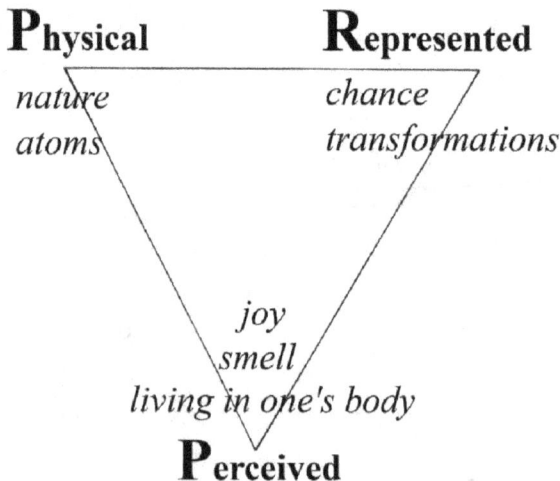

Physical   **Represented**

nature   *chance*
atoms   *transformations*

joy
smell
living in one's body
Perceived

The materialist universe is composed of the following three realities:

Physical: Nature made up of atoms and emptiness. This reality is physical in the sense that it is material.

Perceived: I can feel my body. I breathe in smells. Joy is the purpose of morality. Good resides in the useful. Man need no longer fear the gods, which are matter. Content yourself with the world such as it is. The only alternative to melancholy is hedonism, that is to say knowing how to care for and live in one's body.

Represented: By Darwin and other modern geneticists who confirm that the world is governed by blind creative forces, namely chance, at the origin of all transformations.

The point of view is a philosopher's rooted in respect for nature.

All in all, Democritus proposed a system connected to physical and sensitive reality, along with knowledge built on intellect. The three approaches seem balanced.

1.2 Plato (427 – 347BCE)

Plato opposed Democritus for essentially social reasons. Democritus doesn't take man and his social organization seriously. Plato belonged to the highest aristocracy in Athens, and tends to preserve and consolidate the advantage of his social position, to the extent of envisaging that the philosopher should naturally run the city for its own good. To this effect he proposes a Republic organized into social classes, and led by a philosopher king. At the academy, Plato received noble students who could pay for their studies. Plato therefore needed to be in possession of the Truth, that Democritus saw as an illusion. The young Plato had Socrates as master for nine years. Together with the Pythagoreans, he examined the soul-body opposition and numbers; with Archytes of Tarente (428-347), the ideal of the philosopher king.

Plato well noted Heraclitus' (576-480BCE) observations according to which the being is eternally in the making, things don't have consistency, everything is moving incessantly, and nothing remains. Everything becomes everything, everything is everything. The flow of generation and death never stops. What is visible becomes invisible, what is invisible becomes visible, day and night are one and the same, there is no difference between what is useful and what is harmful.

Nothing is therefore rather this than that, but everything becomes it. Things are never achieved but are being continually created by the forces from which these phenomena flow. Things are assemblies of opposite forces, and the world is a mixture, which must be stirred continuously so that they appear.

Note that in India the Buddha of the same era (563-480 BCE) said the same things as Heraclitus.

These observations were very uncomfortable for Plato, who didn't see the possibility of establishing a truth on impermanence, since what is true now will no longer be an instant later, or in another place, whether it be to interpret nature or laws. For Plato we must go from knowledge as a simple point of view, to the Truth.

Plato therefore constructs a system of concepts and interpretations of the world, metaphysical, and beyond nature. The Forms are the hypothesis of realities that are intelligible, immaterial, immutable, universal, and independent from thought.

When we observe Plato's system, we can only be struck by the fact that our representations are in fact fantasies and, stranger still, that this system has for such a long time been part of our beliefs, which seemed indestructable for so long, like all beliefs.

Platonist idealism, which has carried on into German idealism, has entered into a system of accepted narratives about the knowledge of the world, identified by Lyotard, and in language games, evoked by Wittgenstein, in which an abstract concept refers to another abstract concept, or a reductive mechanical image.

In such an impasse Socrates says, "what makes a thing beautiful…is the presence or the communication of that beauty in itself." (Phaedo). We are in an abstract and transcendental world.

Democritus and Plato have nevertheless several points in common. A soul exists, mortal for Democritus, eternal for Plato. The only true knowledge is not from the senses but from intellect. We are not aware of all our sensations. At any rate the two philosophers are challenged by nature's impermanence and both feel the need to deploy a system of explanation of the world to recover their serenity, unlike Buddha in the same era, who isn't looking for a way of explaining the world, but the right behaviour. As a matter of fact, Buddha accepts permanence and vacuity such as they are, and makes do with distancing himself from the world, to find the path which spares suffering. Democritus invents materialist atomism, deducing that there is no need to fear the gods, or pain, or death. Plato creates an metaphysical system of concepts, which help the philosopher king to lead the city towards the Beautiful and the Good, that is however, still to be defined, and as much as Platonist fantasies will be borne by men, will remain the origin of religious wars.

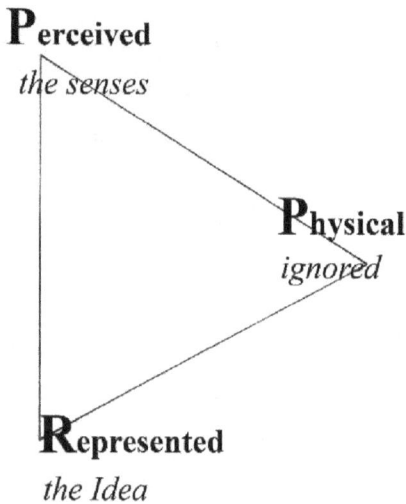

Perceived
the senses

Physical
ignored

Represented
the Idea

The Platonist idealist world offers us three realities:

Physical: This reality is absent with Plato; it is overshadowed by The Forms.

Perceived: I have senses but I must be careful because they don't give me reliable or stable data.

Represented: The world is illuminated with immutable and universal Ideas. Plato supposed rather a demiurge whose relationships with The Forms was not specified, and which produce the soul of the world. Plato gives us a poetic myth. The notion of the soul remains unclear.

The point of view is an aristocratic philosopher king's. The aristocrat's particularity is to have always existed, being right, not having to justify anything at all except to demonstrate that he is at the centre of the system. It refers to noble and idealistic principles, which allow him to justify his power and his superiority.

All in all, Plato's approach seems unbalanced, and revealing of the authoritarian education, in the sense that it introduces unjustifiable aristocratic concepts.

1.3 Aristotle (370 – 322 BCE)

What was young Aristotle going to do to make his way, faced with materialist and idealist schools of thought?

Aristotle's father was doctor to King Amyntas II of Macedonia. Later Aristotle will be like his father in the Macedonian court, but as young Alexander the Great's private tutor.

In 366 BCE Aristotle entered the Academy for twenty years of study with his master Plato. Twice he was in the ranks to succeed him at the head of the Academy. Unsuccessful, he created his own school, which is called the Lyceum.

Although he is a foreigner, Aristotle remained very attached to Athens and to his master's teaching, which supported him brilliantly. Aristotle contested the Ideas theory, but on the whole consolidated Plato's work by becoming interested in a number of scientific and social questions, and by developing rhetoric - that is to say, the art of argumentation.

Aristotle's scientific thinking is unlike that of Democritus. The presuppositions of the two philosophers are contradictory. Democritus sees a world run by blind chance; Aristotle, by a divine spirit.

Plotinus (205-270), Saint Augustin (354-430), Averroes (1126-198) transmitted Plato and Aristotle's teachings to the Middle Ages. Plotinus, born in Lycopolis in Egypt, developed the fantasy of One creator of intellect and soul, whose places, outlines and contents remain vague. The body is reduced to a "tomb" prison of the soul.

Saint Augustin of Hippo in Algeria, conceived of a strong God and the weight of sin. He insisted on the will of God. Wisdom is the gift of God.

Averroes, an Andalusian Muslim doctor, uses the image of the divine craftsman, and of eternal and universal intelligence, in which all men participate. Averroes acknowledges several types of awareness: awareness by intellect and higher awareness in the image of the prophet. However, he pleads the use of reason to better understand the words of the prophet. Removed from his duties as judge but pardoned by the Sultan of Morocco, this scholar had to, as will be the case for Galileo, maintain a careful language.

Represented
music, rhetoric, theater, metaphysics,
ontology, logic, biology,
physics, cosmology

Perceived
ignored

Physical
ignored

At first glance, Aristotle's three worlds seem more balanced than his master Plato's. Yet we notice the predominant weight of the *logos*, the argument to the detriment of perceived feeling and physical reality. The physical world doesn't exist in the sense that Aristotle doesn't breathe, and doesn't seem to have any need of material exchange with nature. As for feeling, his perception reduces itself to discourse on perception. Let us recapitulate these three worlds.

Represented: Physics, biology, Aristotle's cosmology are only discourses of representation, along with metaphysics or logic. Experimentation has not been born.

Perceived: Perception of the world is a discourse on sensitive perception, music, theatre.

Physical: At that time there are no optical instruments making it possible to observe the micrometric world or space, the physical world can only be described carefully, let alone be reached.

The point of view is a Platonist scholar's seeking to review human awareness, but man is overshadowed by the divine. Aristarchus' (310—230 BCE) Greek astronomic science could only reappear with the Polish Copernicus (1473-1543).

1.4   Critique of premodernity

In 529 the Christian Roman emperor Justinian, who wanted to put an end to Pagan philosophy, closed 'The Lycée'. But Aristotle's thinking had a lasting influence on the Roman Empire, St Augustin, Averroes, and the Sorbonne, where, until the German idealists, the mysteries of religion were explained by the logos,.

Christian thinking flourished on the ideas of the emancipation of peoples at the time of the decline of Rome and materialistic thinking, to its emergence in Renaissance times.

However, from the end of Rome, when slavery was replaced by servitude, to the Renaissance, the absence of significant technical progress gave no basis for a revival of debate. All materialist writings, wrongly called pre-Socratic in the aim of denigrating them, were carefully burned in Seville, along with their heretics. Since Democritus, the body had been carefully forgotten; unpredictable nature has been put aside. Christian power's totalitarian system of thinking "was built on a large black hole", according to the expression of Beckett by Jean Anouilh.

What is noteworthy, in the light of current neuro-psychological studies, is the fact that healthy people, as well as patients, suffering from a pathology, firmly believe in their fabrication. It is all the more unshakeable since they have no material element to bring them back to reality, except their taste for power, in the context of the past history of the people.

We can observe that the subject is not aware of the ridiculousness of his fabrication: "I am convinced it is him" says a neighbour suspecting his neighbour.

Someone who fabricates consciously verbalizes it, yet without actually understanding the content, and all the consequences for himself or those around. Our random neuronal connections produce images which feed our multiple and ever new fabrications. Belief, fiction, utopia, are also our mental freedom and our personality. Fabrications are our perceived reality allowing us to make sense of things, and to protect ourselves from the blind brutality of nature. Yet this meaning must be communicated to others in order to live in society.

Instead of doubting or modifying our opinions, we continue to rely on a belief all the stronger, as we have created the conditions so as not to challenge it. Consequently, certain subjects are taboo in a society and prejudices are reinforced.

We can't see what is in front of our eyes. This characteristic is not only a simple system of physical defense, but also the fruit of the process of our biological system, which predicts the future with a minimum of elements. We don't understand what we have before our eyes because we imagine the objects otherwise.

We believe that we are aware of everything all around us, including when we are fooled by a conjurer's tricks. Such a person knew how to distract our attention at the moment when he puts a card up his sleeve.

Our inner conviction is that we can see everything. In believing in the Book, God is made in the image of man, and sees everything. The one who doesn't see the ball is the laughing stock of the other players.

How can we admit to having spent a part of our life in an imaginary universe?

It is something very difficult which requires a revolution in one's conception of the world and in one's idea of Self. Antonio Damasio explains why such a transformation is biologically problematic, due to the fact that our internal register representing the Self belongs to the primitive layers of our brain. According to Penfield (1891-1976), from a very young age, we have acquired a certain conception of the possibilities of the world, we have imagined our strategy and our positioning, in order to survive and conquer. Emotion has etched our experiences in us. From these we have deduced unwavering dogmas.

I am therefore ripe for a world such as it should be perceived and interpreted in the light of my dogmas.

Such is the madness of power. Yet power, by the weight of the administration founded on the hope and terror, stifles life and in turn sees itself asphyxiated.

Renan (1823-1892) notes, "We were expecting Christ and it was the Church which came." Thus the density of Messianic expectation had the weight of institutions of power as a response.

Power divided and isolated, forbidding certain thoughts and full of repressive rules. Roman, Byzantine, German, English rivalries weakened the Roman Catholic system. Technological developments brought astronomy and the New World, thus again challenging imposed beliefs.

Yet today, in the rubble of the Ancient libraries, we rediscover a constellation of great wise men.

Anaximander of Miletus (610-546) attempted to describe and

explain the origin and organization of all aspects of the world from a scientific point of view.

Thales from Miletus (625-547BCE) was a philosopher, scientist, author of a theorem and predicts an eclipse.

Pythagorus of Samos (580-495BCE) was a philosopher, author of a famous theorem.

Heraclitus (576-480BCE) contemporary of Buddha (563-480BCE), Lao Tseu (570-490BCE) and Confucius (555-479BCE), confirms the impermanence of things.

Parmenides (510-450 BCE) maintains that the Earth is at the centre of the universe, and that the living being is a physical reality, complete and spherical.

Anaxagoras (500-428 BCE) taught that the Moon (made from the Earth) reflected the light of the sun, which is a hot stone. Condemned to death as an atheist, he withdrew to Asia minor, where he died.

Empedocles (490-430BCE) was a philosopher, engineer and doctor for whom blood determines thought. We are animals.

Zeno from Elea (480-420BCE), thought that time is not divisible, and supported the tortoise paradox.

Antiphon from Athens (480-410 BCE) invented psychology and the helping relationship recently described by Rogers (1902-1987).

Democritus from Abdera (460-370 BCE) invented the atomic theory.

Plato (427-347 BCE) developed the notion of Idea and The Forms and aspired to the position of philosopher king of the city.

Aristarchus of Samos (310-230BCE) described Copernicus' system (1473-1543) and calculated the distances between the Earth and Moon, and Earth and the Sun.

Euclid (325-270 BCE) in his optical essay, distinguished between the represented world and the perceived world.

Archimedes (287-212 BCE) invented physics and deals with Pi in his work *"Measurement of a circle."*

Eratosthenes (276-194BCE) calculated the Earth's circumference.

Apollodorus of Damascus (60-130)ce builds his Trajan column with its frieze in trigonometric optical illusion.

The subsequent importance given to Plato appeared unjustified from a more advanced study of the input from ancient philosophers. The Christians who attempted to rank all the materialist scholars among the pre-Socratic, and therefore pass off as savage barbarians with unclear thinking, over their esteemed Plato.

Chapter 2
Modernity

2.1 Evolution

Modernity stretches from the Renaissance to the 1960s. At the time of the Renaissance, the confidence of the faithful of the Roman Church was shaken by the discovery of America (1492), the invention of the printing press (1454), Pope Leo X's (1513) wholesale trade in indulgences to construct the new basilica in Rome, the religious Reform (15th century in England and 16th in Germany), and the trial of Galileo (1633).

From the time of the Renaissance, the Earth was no longer at the centre of the Cosmos and Rome is no longer at the centre of the Earth.

An all-powerful reason emerged in the Century of Light. The sciences pursue their glorious march related in the *Encyclopedia*. Kant (1724-1804) put man in his finitude back at the centre of the cosmos. With Auguste Comte (1798-1857) the reason of man became sovereign and master of the world.

Traditional taboos fell one by one: Vesalius did an autopsy in 1543, births are mastered at the end of twentieth century. Yet humanism saw itself reduced to man distanced from his environment, then from man to economic man.

From nineteenth century man has been torn from his natural environment and exploited as a tool by anonymous corporations, international structures opaque to the eyes of elected governments. Man, tied to machines, became a simple element in production and a variable in economic adjustment.

According to Georg Simmel, the autonomous development of law, money and intellectuality are characteristic of modern times. According to Emile Durkheim, in western countries the economy and financial logic of Christian salvation has been turned into pure economics.

The financial worth of a society doesn't at any point take into account the value of operational teams or the managers who coordinate them. The capital results report decides the lot of billions of families. The twentieth century could only be a century of social crisis.

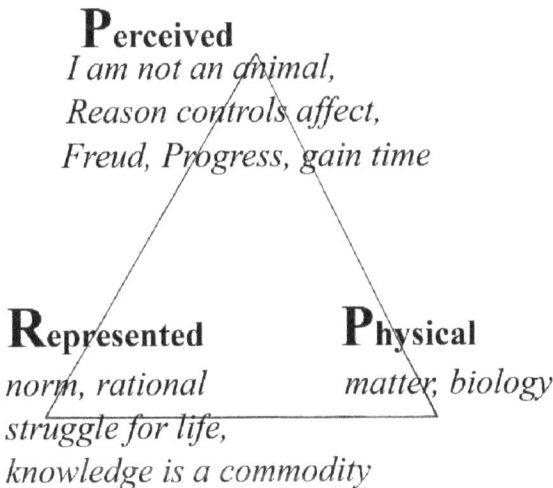

Perceived
I am not an animal,
Reason controls affect,
Freud, Progress, gain time

Represented
norm, rational
struggle for life,
knowledge is a commodity

Physical
matter, biology

The Individual in the modern world.
The person is separated from his natural environment, divided and specialized under the projectors of analytic reason. These changes are called progress owing to increases in life expectancy.

Representation: To be efficient, the modern individual has to be rational, handle speech, be aligned with the puritan norm and knowledge, and if it is useful, it should be purchasable.

Perception: The individual doesn't perceive himself as an animal, his sensations must be controlled, his body and the whole of nature are his servants. The individual must survive on his own and is not society's responsibility. Progress. Productivity. Reduction in time. Freud responded to the traumatisms of this era.

Physics: Biology makes it possible to intervene physically in the world of bacteria. Physics elaborates new materials. We access the cosmos by going to the Moon. Nature is plundered.

The point of view is a bodiless individual in the conquest of the infinitely small to infinitely large physical world.

2.2 Excesses of Modernity

The idea of salvation is either a communist utopia, the national-socialist millenarianism or the riskless society of liberalism, protected by Adam Smith's invisible hand.

Religions of all sorts are machines, which prevent thought. We massacre each other in the name of abstract principles, in the name of a better tomorrow.

We have lived through the totalitarian consequences of the fantasy of the One, of God, of Truth, of Purpose, of the meaning of History. Thus the reference to humanity or to the greatest number, conceals the reference to concrete any concrete individual.

Imperious morality manages the existence of individuals in

reciprocal exchanges, but the economics of salvation has become progressively financial.

Securing existence by fully comprehensive insurance leads to accounting for each instant, to domination by the money king, to productivism, to the consumer society.

Morals give us principles to follow, but for the conservation of the dominant class in power. It is the dichotomous morality of power.

The salvation economy leads to pure economics.

The strongest law rules: those of capital and the financial.

Man is reduced to economic man.

All in all, the rational eliminates affect and turns man into a suffering robot.

With Montesquieu (1689-1755) political power was structured into three bodies: legislative, executive and judiciary. The aim of this utopia was to limit the abuses of royal absolutism. But it resulted in controlling the people with an administration, which was costly, stifling, irresponsive, Kafkaesque, all-powerful and dehumanizing.

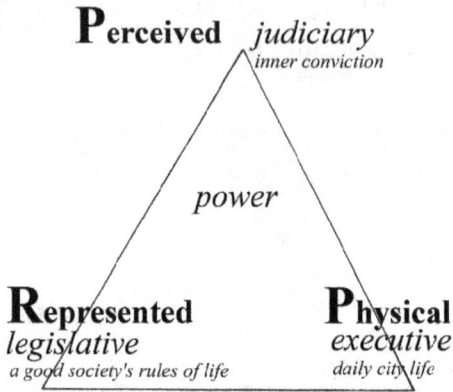

Chapter 3
The Postmodern Reaction

Social evolution has reversed our approach to realities. What has become of these realities today? We are surprised by violent social phenomena when apparently everyone has their place in society. We do not understand not only the car fires, but also the assaults on the police providing security. Even more astounding are the firefighters who come to extinguish fires and rescue people in distress. Giant *aperitifs* are a new binge drinking phenomenon in France, peaceful and anonymous, though not without dangers, the people who participate are more sympathetic but still this testifies to the isolation of man, a cry of alarm in our society. Power seeks, as power always does, to control this excess of affect which is not part of the usual reasonable discourse and which is often of a grotesque logic.

The youth of the sixties in western countries denounced their parents' disappointing modern experiments and expressed, if not reproach, then at least the following:

1. Rational and critical freethinking become inquisitorial dogmas.
2. Only one aspect of being has been highlighted.
3. The individual is no longer capable of living in his body, he can no longer sing, do sport, dance, draw.
4. Power is disconnected from people's reality. Institutions are antiquated; whether they are academies, schools, trade unions, political parties, religious brotherhoods, they are static organizations.
5. Politicians promise, yet the situation deteriorates, resulting

in a feeling of abandonment and lack of interest in the life of the City.

6. The person on the street pays for the excesses of invisible and evasive financial criminals.

From this point forward messages circulate instantaneously. In a disenchanted and absurd world, primacy is given to emotion, to the sensitive, to the tribe, to happiness experienced here and now in the moment. The binge drinking sessions, raves, ritual dances, performances, internet messages, seem to make sense.

3.1 The sociologists' postmodernity

Our postmodern society, established in the 1960s, has a way of functioning which is no longer that of a modern society. We are living in a time of reversal similar to the Renaissance, during which tools of a new order have appeared: globalization, the planet's limited resources, pollution, overpopulation, digital technologies, nano-technologies, relativistic and quantum physics, neurosciences, genetics, stem cells, epigenetics, weapons of mass destruction, mass media, advances in paleontology and anthropology, high-speed trains, Airbus, space rockets, satellites and drones.

World wars and genocides have caused rapid and massive migration that sometimes disrupts social balance. The autonomous individual, triumphant reasoning, and hierarchical power are no longer core values.

Many young graduates can't find work. Population integration, strangers to their languages and their notion of the world and society, emphasizes the social mosaical phenomenon, the administrations in place having difficulties being efficient and being heard.

In the face of this dismantling of the old society still taught in our schools, modern man has lived stoically through the surprises that nature had in store for him. Yet traditional references are slowly being covered in dust.

The new world to come to terms with is indeed the one that Heraclites and Democritus imagined beforehand. Nature is impermanent, we may then have to learn to live in this unpredictable world that nature is offering us.

A new society is emerging, more united, more respectful of the environment, more capable of adapting to the unknown, where links and interactions are more important than the material elements, which make up the physico-biological reality.

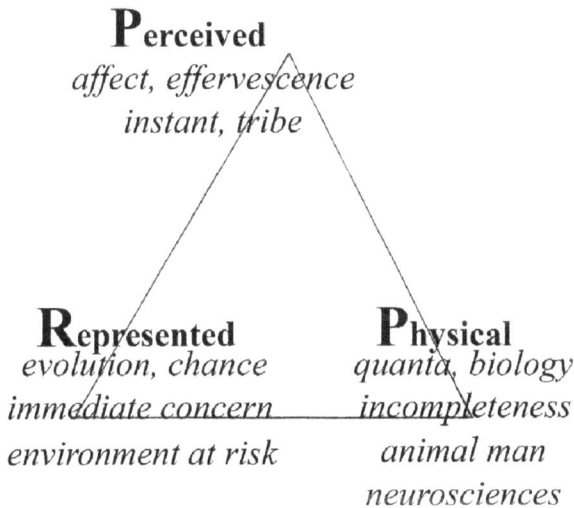

Perceived
affect, effervescence
instant, tribe

Represented
evolution, chance
immediate concern
environment at risk

Physical
quanta, biology
incompleteness
animal man
neurosciences

How does postmodern man live?

Perception: Postmodern man perceives his affects, in the moment, his tribe, his emotions, his emotions shared in an outward and return journey able to go on until the effervescence of a crowd.

Representation: He represents the world in evolution, submitted to constant laws of chance, which involves acting in case of an immediate concern. He knows that the environment is in danger and that it isn't possible to make long term or even medium-term plans.

Physically: The nature of the material world is quantic, random, the notion of time is relative, and the logic we use brings incompleteness.

Neuroscience and paleontology confirm that we belong to the reign of the living being and that we are subjected to its laws, in particular developing to the detriment of our natural and social environment. Our brain itself experiences its development independently.

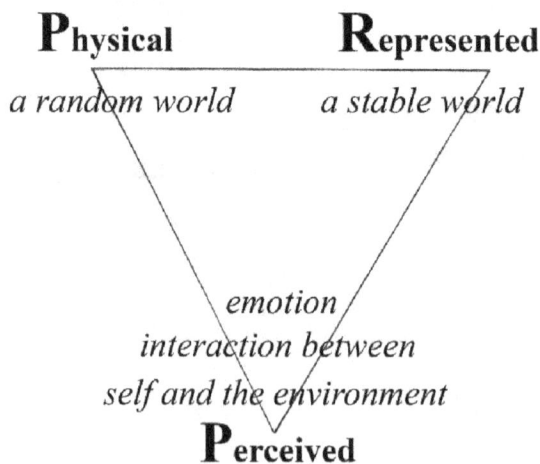

Physical   **R**epresented

a random world   *a stable world*

emotion
interaction between
self and the environment
Perceived

The point of view is a sociologist's who sees a man of flesh seeking to situate himself in order to survive.

3.2 Postmodernity in neuroscience

How does postmodern man function?

The aim of neuroscience is to identify and understand how thought substrates function. Thought is a group of cerebral activities which express themselves in decision, planning, perception, representation and which can take place consciously or unconsciously.

Physically: the body presents the functioning of a system in a random physico-chemical world.

Perception: is first of all an emotion. Emotion is my homeostatic imbalance in the presence of an Object or the Other. The Object changes me chemically by its sole presence.

The Representation: which we have of the world is nevertheless that of a stable world to be able to develop our scenarios in anticipation which allow us to make a decision in time.

The point of view is a neuroscientist's. The mind is an emergence of the body and the body can't function without the mind.

3.3   Postmodern philosophers

In art schools it is customary to cite Deleuze, Derrida and Foucault. All three show that reason is relative, that it is not the royal road leading to knowledge. Deleuze shows that a difference is never reabsorbed in rationality, in rigid concept. Derrida emphasizes the fact that there is a contradiction between philosophies which claim to reach the truth and that human culture is a disjointed network of writings and markings whose author is absent. Foucault shows that knowledge is modified and determined by the exertion of power.

Yet the evolution of ideas is also made under pressure from scientific discoveries by scholars whose culture makes a convergence of cross-disciplinary points of view possible.

Thus the physician Néel has been able to use in a wave Einstein and de Bohr's contributions. The neurologist Damasio rediscovered Spinoza's homeostasis concept and demonstrates that Descartes and German idealists were mistaken in imagining an independent reason for emotion. The biologist Jacques Monod takes up Democritus' role of chance and Carnot's second principle of thermodynamics as motor in the form of a protein.

Finally links between astrophysics, prebiotics, organic chemistry, genetics, biology, paleontology are now established in a global vision of the world and of living being development; these different fields of science continue to make advances in their respective domains.

We are witnessing a decompartmentalization of knowledge between different branches of research at the same time as the development of enhanced specialization. Philosophers accompany chaotically but sometimes originally the explosion of scientific knowledge and intermingling of globalization.

French art schools remain sometimes fearful and don't give the impression of participating in the vital postmodern turbulence. At most they are cultivating their fantasies.

Remarks on Part V
How to live today?

Homer shows us that the right life, far from excessiveness, consists in living harmoniously with the Cosmos.

Baruch Spinoza offers us his meditations for a world of happiness and freedom which could be translated as follows:

Marvel that things be.
Love what we have.
Love the uniqueness of things, of the irreplaceable.
Experience singularity without trying to extract it from its environment.
Get to know the world better, respect different opinions.
The more we are familiar with the world the more joyful we are.
Exist in word and deed.

The sociologist Michel Maffesoli attempted to re-enchant our modern world at the end of his life by leaving us some reflections of wisdom, in particular the following from his last lesson at the Sorbonne:

Say what is, what is seen, what is imagined instead of imagining the One, a Truth, a Purpose, a Sense of History.
Use living notions instead of abstract concepts.
Know how to tune into the tender and cruel reality of things.
Implement multiple knowledge.
Observe the polyhedral aspect of values, grasp truths experienced.
Consider animals, plants, beings, nature.
Consider man's creativity without quality and without speech.

Love is not a sin.
Things are what they are.

Nowadays we also need, in my view, reflecting the postmodern reaction, to understand our present as a dynamic present, in other words re-learn how to link the present to the past and to the future, considering that our legacy is indeed the result of a long succession of innovations which enabled our fathers to compose with the present and imagine the future as far as possible.

Youngsters from the suburbs practicing Hip Hop in a dance hall.

Hip Hop Street
Dancer 4.
24.04.2013.
Thumbnail sketch.
Felt tip pen on
ordinary white A4
80g paper.
Xavier Bolot.
This drawing is
neither a photo
nor a series of
stills.

Hip Hop street
dancer 3.
24.04.2013.
Thumbnail sketch.
Felt tip pen on
ordinary white A4
80g paper.
Xavier Bolot.
This drawing is
neither a photo nor
a series of stills.

Epilogue

1 Decompartmentalize thought

The wonder is that music exists in its evasive precision. Music doesn't explain, it tells the world, it is jubilant, it involves us. It is, by its very existence, proof that we can access a world without speech. For Clément Rosset, only music allows us to accept the world.

If we could in fact at some point find ourselves under the dominant influence of a particular emotion, however our life is made up of multi-sensorial emotions that our brain and our body deal with in parallel in order to pursue action.

Speech is only a tribe's instrument of communication that feels the need to organize itself in order to survive and consequently construct a central nervous system that will be in possession of power. Speech is polysemic, the ritual phrase triggers obedience, confirming movement and facial expression.

Our body is a physical reality of the world, it is immersed in the material world from which behaviour, thought and action emerge. All these phenomena work in constant interaction and form a vital entity. Certain wise men understood that. Juvenal recommended "A healthy mind in a healthy body" *(Satires, X356)*. Spinoza writes in Ethics, "An idea which excludes the existence of our body can only be found in our Mind but it is contrary to it." *(Ethics, III from nature of affects, proposal X)*.

The abstract ideology of the truth and its horde of sacred destructions have only existed to satisfy primitive pulsions of power.

2 What becomes of art?

Contemporary art is composed of many very diverse movements borne by a great number of innovative and courageous artists. The institutions in power, in ignorance and conservatism, only recognize a few of them. Let us cite mainly commercial art and conceptual art.

Commercial art conducts financial investments in movable assets which evade tax, an organization of quotation of commercial objects making it possible to guarantee the investments, no matter the object.

Conceptual art is another phenomenon, established at the beginning of the twentieth century, from the idea that any object can be an object of art as long as we know how to state it brilliantly. It is the art of ordinary madness. This movement which sees itself as avant-garde has been petrified for a long time, disabled at birth, deprived of its senses, reinventing the moon, ignoring conceptual displacements already invented 7000 years ago by Sumer's accountants when they invented the first abacus.

Content with itself, the purpose of conceptual art in France today is to justify the payment of officials who take no risks, at the expense of the nation, and whose main worry is to survive by making illusions. It is time to put away Diafoirus.

Artists of the conceptual movement still haven't understood concepts introduced a century ago by physicists attempting to mock a world exploding with energy around them. Lost, they take refuge in discourse and derision.

Strangers to the world, they are incapable of mobilizing their bodies. Official contemporary exhibitions with a tendency towards conceptual art are too often sinister, boring, deprived of imagination and zest for life, using the same clichés.

Unfortunately, some art schools still grant an excessive part to the conceptual movement. Although there are brilliant teachers and active young artists, a considerable number of professors pervade in amateurism and don't know with excellence how to either draw, paint, play a musical instrument, recite, dance, use electronics, photographic or cinematographic techniques, or sculpt, or handle earth, or cook it.

They are reduced to making speeches about the absence of work, but their gibberish does not allow them to publish writings that are worthy of their hegemonic pretentions.

France let impressionist works go to the USA at the beginning of the twentieth century. France, in the person of Jack Lang, who, haunted by regret, created in 1982 'Les FRACS' (Regional Contemporary Art Foundation) to save possible new French masterpieces, but, not having much to store, we witnessed the opaque assembly of a jumble of conceptual works which are covered in dust through a lack of interest. The system is incapable of reforming itself. In 1970 we went from one academism to another, from a classical vision of stereotyped bodies to a Platonist prudish and discarnate conceptual vision of the body. Other capitals in the world take the reins of a diverse and creative cultural vitality.

Groups of researchers are working to change this situation. They are not, of course, part of outdated schools, official learned institutions antiquated on the inside and cracked under outside evolution. They get in through the obscurantist cracks in the walls to accelerate their inevitable downfall and to offer new learning styles. New approaches are being examined, in France at GREAS (research group on Artistic and Society Eco training), as part of CEAQ (centre for studies on the present and everyday) René Descartes University – Sorbonne Paris V, or else in Montpellier, in Grenoble, but also in Spain in Granada, in Brazil in Rio and in a large part of the country, or even still in Britain and Canada.

No thought can be coherent without taking into balanced consideration the three aspects of physical, perceived and represented reality. No art can be mastered if the body can't adopt gestures necessary for its creation.

An effort of pluri-disciplinary and skilled culture in at least the scientific field should be undertaken to train artists to keep up with life and integrate them with participants of the century.

Our young artists should in parallel learn to inhabit their bodies, to listen to it, to listen to the world, to live in symbiosis with it. Then they will be able to work on understanding the world, from the biological cell to the galaxies, to researching their own coherence.

Immersed in the world they will be able, with the help of chance, to bring their contribution to human creation.

Annexes

I The limits of logic

In daily life we realize the limits of the efficiency of logic to run our life or else to quite simply survive. When we are suddenly confronted with a new face, we don't have a file containing an interview, a curriculum, a graphology, a criminal record, a family tree, all of the things that would reassure an employer. I should then, in this case, react as I feel and thus rely on my best guide which I call intuition.

When we want to be sure of our civil rights, we plunge ourselves into 'les petits Dalloz' (a law book), which is no longer at all 'petit' (small) as it has quadrupled in size between 1970 and 2010. The cross-referencing of amended articles in deleted and new articles make it a complete jungle. The same applies to labor laws and we are led to incoherences such as: for working on a Sunday in a supermarket, a judgement from the Courts of Appeal in 2013 is openly contested by all the citizens, workers, management and customers concerned. This incoherence of logic is inevitable, on the basis that logic, depends on the strongest lobby.

In the field of so-called hard science, physicists have discovered that radioactive bodies, but also a considerable number of elements, have random electromagnetic behaviour. In other words they are relevant to the domain of probability calculation.

This is puzzling because we believe that we are not involved with this kind of phenomenon in everyday life, although, if we think about it we will discover, like Darwin, that on a macroscopic scale, chance is king.

This was also Einstein and de Bohr's debate. The former, supporting the vision of a determinist world while the latter observed that chance is everywhere.

In our western culture there are many who do not want to lose their traditional points of reference. Often we still want to believe that the world is determine; it reassures us and allows us to anticipate by wagering on an extrapolated continuity of events.

Schrödinger attempted to explain this misunderstanding with a fairy tale, the one with the cat in the quantum universe. But we will see that we only result in contradictions of our own logic.

2 Schrödinger's cat

Schrödinger imagined the cat experiment in 1935 to illustrate difficulties brought by the probabilistic concept introduced in so-called quantum mechanics. We are at the beginning of the quantum adventure.

Quantum mechanics describe the probabilistic world of matter to a microscopic scale. Physics experimentation indisputably confirms this aspect of matter.

In quantum mechanics the microscopic world is described in terms of probabilities and classical determinism no longer exists. We can no longer speak about the position of a particle, but only the probability of it finding itself in a specific place. This concept is rather strange, in any case very far from our experience of everyday life even if we feel the constant presence of chance in daily events: we play at lotto, we meet a friend in the street that we weren't expecting to see, we hear that there has been an accident, an earthquake, that an athlete has won the title of champion of the world by a hundredth of a second, that a painter at an auction has cleared an unexpected and enormous amount. Furthermore, in everyday life, we use electronic devices functioning with materials whose behaviour we know is random.

This therefore raises the question of knowing if the indeterminism which rules the microscopic world can also rule the macroscopic world.

If it is possible to admit that the microscopic world is ruled by quantum laws, it seems more difficult when we speak about everyday life. Where is the incoherence? Schrödinger's mental experiment has been imagined precisely to make microscopic indeterminism emerge into the macroscopic world of our daily life. Schrödinger's idea consists of putting a cat into a closed box, though any animal can be used since it concerns a thought experiment. This box is equipped with a system destined to kill the cat. The system is composed of a flask of poison, a small quantity of radioactive matter and a Geiger counter. When the first disintegration of a radio-active nucleus is produced, the Geiger counter reacts by triggering a mechanism which breaks the flask and frees the lethal poison. Thus the disintegration of a radioactive nucleus, a microscopic process, manifests itself by the death of the cat, a macroscopic event.

The disintegration of a radio-active nucleus is a purely quantum process which is described in terms of probabilities. It is impossible to predict which nucleus will transform itself first or, otherwise, when the first disintegration will happen. The only thing that we can calculate is the probability that a certain number of nuclei have disintegrated after a given time. Let us choose a radioactive substance so that after five minutes there is a fifty percent chance that the nucleus has disintegrated and a fifty percent chance that nothing has happened. Let us close the box and wait for five minutes. Since the radio-active disintegration expresses itself in terms of probabilities, the cat's lot can only be described in similar terms. After five minutes, there is therefore a fifty percent chance that the cat is dead and a fifty percent chance that it is alive.

In quantum mechanics, the cat is therefore neither dead nor alive. Its a poetic image and fantasmatic. It is only when we finally open the box that one of the two possible states become the "reality." The cat will therefore be either alive or dead.

It is possible to imagine that a particle finds itself in an uncertain state, each affected by a certain probability, since nobody can see for a particle what consequences that involves on a microscopic scale which is not ours. However, this becomes very difficult when we consider a macroscopic object like the cat in question. The idea of an animal neither dead nor alive but in a state of incertitude is rather difficult to accept, even though, for example, some believers imagine that their dead continue to watch over them.

Coming back down to Earth. In fact, by opening the box, we go from the imagined to the experienced, from the represented to the perceived. The only logical reasoning has no chance of removing the paradox by remaining in the rational represented imaginary world.

In wanting to know by thought about the state of the cat, the researcher anticipates the moment at which the box will be open, holds back time. Thus, as Bergson observed in his *Essay on immediate data from consciousness*, the scientist combines the past, present and future, and by that, quantity and quality.

As the physician Jean-Pierre Cohen-Addad underlines, "It is absurd today to want to transpose submicroscopic physics to our macroscopic scale. Some have their minds stuck in classical mechanics and its determinism in the absence of friction. The passage from classical physics to quantum physics occurs naturally when quantum numbers become very large leading to a continuity which no longer require quantification. The results of quantum mechanics are checked on a macroscopic scale and the MRI seems very useful in the medical world."

3 The three realities of communication

In applied psychology, Transactional Analysis has attempted to describe the nature of spoken transactions between two people. The founder of this is Eric Berne of MacGill University in Montreal, Quebec. Since then a number of works have been published on this theme in the world and a great many seminars have been followed by company management personnel to improve communication in work teams.

After that, gestology became interested in conscious and unconscious gestural and corporal transactions between individuals. What is it concerned with? The idea of Transactional Analysis consists of saying that each of us is made up of three people: the Child, the Adult, and the Parent.

The Child feels emotions, takes refuge, attacks, wants to laugh, to cry, asks for help, or thinks he can govern everything. He is on the Earth in the sense that he feels his body which produces in him an awareness of a scenario that he doesn't always manage to situate, not yet having forged a coherent system of explanation of the world.

The Parent represents authority, tradition, customs, points of reference, the "it must be done like that" morality, principles etched in our memory by familial society or extended society, the "if you don't want to get into trouble", the "don't do that", "arrive on time" "be careful."

The Adult speaks like a computer, only considers pure and simple concrete facts, on solid ground, and, from there, looks for balanced solutions.

The point of this distinction of three psychological beings which form a personality is to easily understand why a conversation can get bogged down when two people are face to face, and, inversely, to which conditions of a conversation make it possible to overcome differences, in order to build agreement. We are therefore at the heart of the study of social bonding.

If the two characters assume the Parents' role, there is a strong chance of agreement. For example, a conversation of the type: "My dear sir, you understand that today it has become impossible!", the other replies, "That's true enough, it's all falling apart" etc.

If the characters both assume the Child's attitude, varied scenarios can manifest, which will all end up staying in the world of childhood: "It's my toy." " Well I'm playing with it."

If the two Adults are speaking, we can witness a fair transaction:
"This against that."
"When?"
"The date"
"Good."

These transactions are horizontal when Child speaks to Child, Adult to Adult, Parent to Parent. But chains of cross-exchanges exist Parent Child, Adult Parent, Adult Child, Parent Adult, etc. Each partner chooses the level of response in which he wants to react at each step.

Transactional Analysis can also appear impressive in the hands of a manipulator. An adult can in fact speak to the Child of the Other to manipulate him, unless the Other changes register to speak as a Parent or Adult.

It is very instructive to follow levels of conversation following the departure points and arrival points Parent, Child, Adult of each of the speakers.

The Child, the Adult and the Parent can be seen as corresponding to the levels of development of the person who is built in successive layers.

Yet, the Child is first sensitive, perceptive; the Adult is the one who is interested in the facts of the physical world leading to a material solution, to follow an action. The Parent is the representative of overhanging morality, of memory and of experience, from the represented world.

Each is made up of several Selfs. However, the communication will be balanced and productive when three aspects have been taken into consideration:

perceived – sensitive,
physical – object of my action,
represented – imagined.

To go further

Sciences

Aglioti, Salvatore, DeSouza, Joseph FX, Goodale, Melvyn A, *Size-constrat illusions deceive eye but not the hand*, Current Biology vol.5 N 6, p 679-685, Cell Press, 30.6.95.

Aristote, *Physique,* Flammarion, 1999.

Aristarque de Samos, voir Thomas L. Heath, *Aristarchus of Samos – The Ancient Copernicus, A history of Greek astronomy to Aristarchus together with Aristarchus, treatise on the sizes and distances of the sun and moon, a new Greek text with translation and notes*, Oxford University Press, 1913.

Averroès, cf Benmaklouf, Ali, *Averroès*, Perrin, 2009.

Bayes, Thomas, voir Dale, Andrew, I., *A theory of Inverse Probability*, Springer, 1999.

Ben-Jacob, Eschel, Levine, Herbert, *Des fleurs de bactéries*, Pour la Science, dossier 44.

Berthoz Alain, *Le Sens du mouvement*, Odile Jacob, 1997.

Berthoz Alain, *La décision*, Odile Jacob, 2003.

Bolot Xavier, *Dessiner en perspective réelle*, L'Harmattan, 2006.

Bolot Xavier, *La lumière neutre*, L'Harmattan, 2009.

Bolot Xavier, *Comment représenter l'action*, L'Harmattan, 2012.

Boole, George, voir Claude, D., Permingeat, N., *Algèbre de Boole*, Masson, 1998.

Borh Niels, *Physique atomique et connaissance humaine*, Gauthier-Villars, 1961.

Chaline Jean, Marchand, Didier, *Les merveilles de l'évolution*, Editions Universitaires de Dijon. 2002.

Cohen, L., Dehaene, S., Naccache, L., Dehaene- Lambertz, G., Henaff, M-A., Michel, F., 2000, *The visual word form area: spatial and temporal* characterisation of an initial stage of reading in normal subjects and *posterior split-brain patients*, Brain 123 (Pt2), p.291-307.

Cohen-Addad, J.P., *Polymères, La matière plastique*, Belin, 2007.

Connes, A., *Géométrie non commutative*, InterEditions, 1990.

Cuvier Georges, *Discours sur les révolutions de la surface du globe et* sur les changements qu'elles ont produits dans le règne animal, Christian Bourgeois, 1985.

Damasio, Antonio, *Le Sentiment même de soi : corps, émotions, conscience*, Odile Jacob, 1999.

Damasio, Antonio, *Spinoza avait raison*, Odile Jacob, 2005.

Dantzer Robert, *Les Emotions*, PUF, *Que sais-je?* 1993.

Darwin Charles, *De l'origine des espèces au moyen de la sélection naturelle ou la lutte pour l'existence*, F. Maspero, 1980.

Démocrite, voir Salem, Jean, *Les Atomistes de l'antiquité*, Flammarion, 2013.

Duve de Christian, *Construire une cellule : Essai sur la nature et l'origine de la vie*, Bruxelles, De Boeck-Wesmael, 1990.

Euclide, *Les Eléments*, PUF, 1994.

Felleman, D.J., Van Essen, D.C., *Distributed hierarchical processing in the primate cerebral cortex*, Cerebral Cortex, 1:1-47, 1991.

Fodor, Jerry A. (1983). *Modularity of Mind: An Essay on Faculty Psychology*. Cambridge, Mass.: MIT Press.

Gazzaniga, M. S., *Principles of human brain organisation derived from split brain studies*, Neuron 14: 217-228, 1995.

Gödel, voir Smullyan, Raymond, *Les théorèmes d'incomplétude de Gödel*, Dunod, 2000.

Haley Jay, *Un thérapeute hors du commun : Milton Erickson*, Declée. Brouwer, Paris, 1984.

Helmholtz, Hermann von, *Théorie physiologique de la musique fondée sur l'étude des sensations auditives*, Ulan Press, 2012.

Hess, Eckhard H.; *The role of pupil size*, Scientific American, April, 1965.

Hess, Eckhard H.; *The tell-tale eye*, Van Nost.Reinhold, U.S., 1975.

Klingler, Cécile, Filloux Alain, Lazdunski, Andrée, *Les biofilms, forteresses bactériennes*, La Recherche, sept 2005.

Kupiec Jean-Jacques, Sonigo Pierre , *Ni Dieu ni gène, pour une autre théorie de l'hérédité*, Paris, Seuil, 2000.

Lai, Sandra, INRS, *La vie sociale des bactéries*, ACFAS 2007.

Laroche S. and Davis S. Jones M.W., Errington M.L., French P.J., Fine A.,

 Bliss T.V.P., Garel S., Charnay P., Bozon B., *A requirement for the immediate early gene Zif268 in the expression of late LTP and the consolidation of long-term memories.* Nature Neurosci., 4: 289-296, 2001.

Lavoisier, voir Querel, Alain, *Antoine Laurent de Lavoisier*, Anovi, 2009.

Lewin Benjamin, *Gènes*, Flammarion 1992.

Margulis, Lynn and Dorion, Sagan, *Slanted Truths: Essays on Gaia, Symbiosis, and Evolution*, Copernicus Books, 1997.

Miller Stanley L. *"A production of amino acids under possible primitive earth conditions"*, Science, vol. 117, no 3046, 1953, p. 528-529.

Monod Jacques, *Le hasard et la nécessité*, Seuil, 1970.

Naccache, Lionel, *Perdons-nous connaissance ?* Odile Jacob, 2010.

Naccache, Lionel, *Le nouvel inconscient : Freud, Christophe Colomb des neurosciences*, Odile Jacob, 2006.

Ninio, Jacques, *La science des illusions*, Odile Jacob, 1998.

Prigogine Ilya, *L'homme devant l'incertain*, Odile Jacob, 2001.

Pythagore, *Les vers d'or*, Adyar, 1998.

Riemann, G.B.F., *Uber die Hypothesen, welche der Geometrie zu Grunde liegen*, Dover, NewYork, 1953.

Shannon E.Claude, *A mathematical theory of communication*, Bell System Technical Journal, vol. 27, p. 379-423 and 623-656, July and October, 1948.

Sutherland John D., Powner Matthew W., Gerland, Béatrice, *Synthesis* of activated pyrimidine ribonucleotides in prebiotically plausible *conditions*, Nature 459, 239-242 (14 May 2009).

Titchener, E.B., *Experimental psychology: A manual of laboratory practice.* (Vol. 1) New York, NY: MacMillan & Co., 1902.

Ungerleider, L., Mishk, M, *Advances in the analysis of visual behaviour*, D. Ingle, M.A. Goodale, R. Mansfield, Boston, MIT Press, p. 549, 1982.

Verstichel, Patrick, Cambier, Jean, *Le cerveau réconcilié, précis de neurologie cognitive*, Masson, 1998.

Weiskrantz, Lawrence, *Blindsight. A case study and implications*, Oxford University Press, 2000.

Whalen, Paul J., et al., *Human amygdalia responsibility to mask fearful eye whites*, Science, 306 (5704), p 2061,2004.

Philosophy and society

Anaxagore, voir Curd, Patricia, *Anaxagoras of Clazomenae Fragments and Testimonia*, University of Toronto Press, 2007.

Anouilh, Jean, *Becket ou l'honneur de Dieu*, Poche, 1972.

Aristote, *Poétique*, PUF, 1990.

Aristote, *Métaphysique*, Flammarion, 2008.

Averroès, *Grand commentaire sur la métaphysique d'Aristote* (livre II, c.a.d. B), trad. L. Bauloye, Paris, Vrin, 2003

Bachelard, Gaston, *La philosophie du non : Essai d'une philosophie du nouvel esprit scientifique.* P.U.F. 1940.

Baudrillard, Jean, *Simulacres et simulation*, Galilée, 1981.

Baudrillard, Jean, Guillaume, Marc, *Figures de l'altérité*, Descartes et Cie, 1994.

Bergson H., *Essai sur les données immédiates de la conscience*, PUF.

Berne, Eric, *Analyse transactionnelle et psychothérapie*, Payot, 1971.

Dali, Salvador, *Google/ Salvador Dali Marché d'esclaves.*

Delaunay voir Schneider et Bernier, *Robert et Sonia Delaunay : naissance de l'art abstrait*, J.-C. Lattès, 1995.

Deleuze, Gilles, Guattari, Félix, *Qu'est-ce que la philosophie?* Les Editions de Minuit, 2005.

Deleuze, Gilles, *Différence et répétition*, PUF, 1968.

Derrida, Jacques, *L'écriture et la différence*, Seuil, 1967.

Durkheim, Emile, *Les règles de la méthode sociologique*, Flammarion, 1999.

Durkheim, Emile, *Les formes élémentaires de la vie religieuse*, PUF.

Eliade, Mircea, *Images et symboles*, essais sur le symbolisme magico-religieux, Gallimard, 1952.

Eliade, Mircea, *Traité d'histoire des religions*, Payot, Paris, 1964.

Ferry, Luc, *Apprendre à vivre-2, la sagesse des mythes*, J'ai Lu, 2009.

Foucault, Michel, *L'archéologie du savoir*, Paris, Gallimard, 1969.

Freud, Sigmund, *Psychopathologie de la vie quotidienne*, Payot, 2004.

Hegel G.W.F., *Phénoménologie de l'esprit*, Gallimard, 1993.

Heidegger, Martin, *Etre et temps*, Gallimard, 1986.

Heidegger, Martin, *Lettre sur l'humanisme*, Aubier, 1957.

Husserl, Edmund, *L'idée de la phénoménologie*, PUF, 2004.

Jousse, Marcel, *L'Anthropologie du geste*, Gallimard, 1974.

Kant, *Critique de la raison pure*, Flammarion, 2006.

Leviant, Isia, web: michaelbach.de/ot/mot_enigma/ý

Leviant, Isia, Exposition permanente Eurêka, Palais de la Découverte.https://tinyurl.com/ybyucjkr

L'Ecclésiaste, *Illusion des illusions*, traduction Jean-Jacques Wahl, DDB, 2011.

Lyotard, Jean-François, *La phénoménologie*, Que sais-je ? , PUF, 1954.

Lyotard, Jean-François, *La condition postmoderne. Rapport sur le savoir,* Editions de Minuit, 1979.

Maffesoli, Michel, *Le temps des tribus*, Le Livre de Poche, 1988.

Maffesoli Michel, *Le réenchantement du monde*, Tempus Philo, Perrin, 2009.

Maffesoli Michel, *La crise est dans nos têtes*, Jacob-Duvernet, 2011.

Maffesoli Michel, *Homo eroticus*, CNRS Editions, 2012.

Merleau-Ponty Maurice, La phénoménologie de la perception*, Gallimard, 1945.*

Messinger, Joseph, *Ces gestes qui trahissent*, First, 2005.

Molière, *Le malade imaginaire*, Hachette, 1999.

Miquel, Paul-Antoine, *Comment penser le désordre ?* Fayard, 2000.

Nierenberg, Gérard, Calero, Henry, *Lisez dans vos adversaires à livre ouvert*, First, 1986.

Nietzsche, Friedrich, *La naissance de la tragédie*, Gallimard, 1967.

Nietzsche, Friedrich, *Le gai savoir*, Gallimard, 1967.

Onfray, Michel, *Contre histoire de la philosophie*, 12 CD Université Populaire de Caen, France Culture- Grasset.

Pastoureau, Michel. *Couleurs, images, symboles*, Le Léopard d'Or, 1993.

Pastoureau, Michel. *Dictionnaire des couleurs de notre temps, symbolique et société*, Bonneton, Paris, 1999.

Pastoureau, Michel, *Bleu, histoire d'une couleur*, Points, Seuil, 2000.

Penfield, Wilder, *The Mystery of the Mind: A Critical Study of Consciousness and the Human Brain,* Princeton Univ. Press, 1975.

Pirandello, Luigi, Arnaud, Michel, *Comme tu me veux*, L'Arche, 1988.

Platon, *Oeuvres complètes*, Flammarion, 2011.

Plotin, *Les ennéades*, Nabu Press, 2010.

Rosset Clément, *L'Objet singulier*, Paris, Éditions de Minuit, 1979.

Sénèque, *Lettres à Lucilius*, Mille et Une Nuits, 2002.

Saint Augustin, *Les confessions*, Flammarion, 1993.

Simmel, Georg, *Philosophie de l'argent*, PUF, 2007.

Spinoza, Baruch, *L'éthique*, Gallimard, 1984.

Voltaire, *Candide ou l'optimisme*, Hachette, 2008.

Weber, Max, *L'éthique protestante et l'esprit du capitalisme*, Pocket.

Varin, Dario, *Fenomeni di contrasto e diffusione cromatica nell'organizzazione del campo percettivo*, Libreria del Riacquisto, 1971.

Wittgenstein, Ludwig, *Le Cahier bleu et le cahier brun*, trad. Marc Goldberg et Jérôme Sackur, Gallimard, 1996.

Wittgenstein, Ludwig, *Recherches philosophiques*, trad. Françoise Dastur, Maurice Élie, Jean-Luc Gautero, Dominique Janicaud, Élisabeth Rigal, Gallimard, 2004.

Index

www.ingramcontent.com/pod-product-compliance
Lightning Source LLC
Chambersburg PA
CBHW050654270326
41927CB00012B/3016